JUSTIFYING BELIEF

Stanley Eugene Fish

JUSTIFYING BELIEF

Stanley Fish and the Work of Rhetoric

Gary A. Olson

Foreword by
Stanley Fish

Afterword by
J. Hillis Miller

State University of New York Press

Published by
State University of New York Press, Albany

For information, address State University of New York Press, 90
State Street, Suite 700, Albany, NY, 12207

Cover art by Denis Sargent, *Perversion of Ancient Elements/Fire
Power*, 1999, dsargent@uwm.edu

Production of this book was assisted by a generous grant from the USF
Publication Council

Production by Diane Ganeles
Marketing by Patrick Durocher

Library of Congress Cataloging-in-Publication Data

Olson, Gary A., date–
    Justifying belief : Stanley Fish and the work of rhetoric /
    Gary A. Olson ; foreword by Stanley Fish ; afterword by J. Hillis Miller.
        p. cm.
    Includes bibliographical references and index.
    ISBN 0-7914-5611-0 (alk. paper)—
    ISBN 0-7914-5612-9 (pbk.: alk. paper)
    1. Fish, Stanley, Eugene—Contributions in rhetoric. 2. English philology—
    Study and teaching. 3. Language and culture. 4. Knowledge, Theory of.
    5. Criticism. 6. Rhetoric. I. Title.

PE64.F57 O47 2002   2002021247
801'.95'092—dc21
        CIP
              10   9   8   7   6   5   4   3   2   1

For Stanley and Jane

who have contributed immeasurably
to the intellectual life
of the academy

Books are not absolutely dead things, but do contain a potency of life in them to be as active as that soul was whose progeny they are; nay they do preserve as in a vial the purest efficacy and extraction of that living intellect that bred them.
—John Milton

His words, like so many nimble and airy servitors, trip about him at command.
—John Milton

By labour and intent study (which I take to be my portion in this life), joined with the strong propensity of nature, I might perhaps leave something so written to after times as they should not willingly let it die.
—John Milton

yet he pleas'd the ear, / And with persuasive accent thus began.
—John Milton

Contents

Foreword

Stanley Fish

Iam honored by the attention Gary Olson and Hillis Miller have paid to my work in this volume, and while I might have small quarrels to pick with a few of the points they make, this is not the place to rehearse them. Rather, I want here to offer a narrative and slightly autobiographical account of how I came to some of the positions they analyze.

When I first began to drive as a teenager growing up in Providence, Rhode Island, I used to travel quite regular routes on my way to and back from the two or three places one might want to get to in that then decaying New England town. One day, while I was stopped at a traffic light, I suddenly realized that I had stopped at that very intersection earlier going in the other direction—and indeed had stopped at it twice daily for many months—but had never quite tumbled to the fact that the morning intersection and the evening intersection (like the morning star and the evening star) were the same. But as I came to the "same" intersection in subsequent days, I began to wonder: well, in what respect exactly are they the same? Nothing about them appeared to be the same when I came upon them on my travels: the buildings to the left and right of me, the streets on which I could turn, the horizon that told me where I was in relation to the house I lived in, the position of the sun, and so on—all were different.

It occurred to me almost immediately that the difficulty, as I had conjured it up, was a function of the fact that my perception (and therefore my experience) of the intersection was angled and partial. If I imagined myself not on the ground but at an elevated height, I would have a bird's-eye or wide-angle lens view of the intersection, and my perception wouldn't be partial, but complete and comprehensive. But no sooner had I resolved the problem than it returned to bedevil me in the form of two new questions. First, a material or physical question. Where exactly would this bird's-eye view be, and how would I get to it? If it were located at the top of one of the buildings surrounding the intersection, it would deliver a perspective no less angled than the ones I occupied on the ground. And if I hovered above the intersection so that I was positioned above its exact center, what would hold me in place while I took my long and impartial look? But then a second question posed itself—one that cut much deeper. Even if I could ascend to the proper height and remain immobile, would not the perspective I had achieved also be partial in that its very refusal to incline in one direction or another removed it from any relationship to the intersection as either planned or encountered? Rather then being a more comprehensive view, the view from above (or as we might put it today, the view from nowhere) would merely be a *different* view—not superior or higher or deeper or truer, just different. And this would be so too, I reasoned, of blueprints, which might in one sense be an accurate representation of the intersection—all the widths, lengths, and angles would be correctly noted—but as a representation it would leave out the feel of the materials, not to mention the feel of the intersection for its users, for those whose relationship to it was purposive. (I pass by, because I didn't think of it then when I was sixteen or seventeen years old, the physicalist reduction of giving an exhaustive material description of the intersection, an inventory of what it was made of; such a description is of course possible, but however exhaustive it might be it would tell us nothing about the intersection as intersection, as something devised to facilitate the flow of traffic and provide opportunities for motorists to branch off from it to various destinations.)

Now, I will not pretend that these juvenile reflections led directly to the arguments of which Olson gives such a full account. In fact, the direction of influence is the other way around: it is in the light of the arguments I later elaborated that it became possible to endow my Rhode Island ruminations with a (retroactive) significance they would otherwise never have had. I did not know then (even in some inchoate, dreamy way) that I would become obsessed with the question of sameness and difference and with the relation between the sign and the signified and with Ferdinand de Saussure's account of language as a "system of differences without positive terms"—a system whose articulations and discriminations are not constrained by something more substantial (which is not to say that there is nothing more substantial, only that whatever it is [God, nature, Reason] language does not reflect it or match itself to it)—and with Derrida's notion of *différance*. All of that lay far in the future; I was just a kid in a car thinking thoughts for the sheer fun of it (how little has changed).

Later, when I had a more professional relation to metaphysical speculations, a chance encounter might immediately be folded into what was becoming a web of ideas. This happened to me once at a cocktail party when my host told the story of a relative (his sister, I think) who, after having undergone a brain operation, became unable to distinguish one table utensil from another. She didn't know a fork from a spoon from a knife from a ladle. Someone remarked that she could easily learn, or relearn, these identifications: just point to each and say in turn fork, knife, spoon, and so on. But that advice assumed that objects present themselves to us directly and that all we have to do is find enough different sounds to attach to each of them. The truth, however (as by then I had come to believe it), is that we know objects diacritically—that is, by their not being other objects, all of which in turn are known (become present for us as distinctive entities) by what they are not. We know a fork as not being a spoon and a spoon as not being a knife and a knife as not being a fork, and we know table utensils (as a category of objecthood) as not being garden implements (although we also know that in certain Robinson Crusoe-like moments things to garden with can become things to eat with). The paradoxical point is that identity is a function of nonidentity, of differential relations. Everything is what it is by virtue of what it is not. Or, in Matthew Kramer's elegant rendering of the Derridian insight,

> *All* units are sheer outcomes of differences, and, exactly for that reason, no units can act as benchmarks that could relieve differences from having to operate as their own foundations. Every unit has to mark itself off from every other unit in order to become present; but squarely because this proposition must apply fully to *all* the units, there cannot be anything present from which anything else can differ. (7)

Taken seriously, and in the years when I was reading Derrida and going to cocktail parties I was taking it very seriously, this argument spells the death of foundationalism, that effort, as old as Plato and as new as the information revolution associated with the Internet, to identify an independent ground in relation to which contextually produced specifications of fact, determinations of meaning, and stipulations of value could be tested and either confirmed or disconfirmed. If there is nothing that is irreducibly (not dependent on any contextual or differential framing) present, nothing whose identification as a thing is self-declaring and universally perspicuous, nothing that is not an effect of a system of differences (without positive terms), then the judgments we make in the context of some such system—a discipline, a political structure, a scientific procedure—cannot be approved or corrected by something that stands outside the system and serves as a fulcrum or reference point.

This is not to say that we cannot settle a dispute by pointing to some fact or invoking some principle or rehearsing the dictum of some authority. We do such things all the time, but if Saussure and Derrida and Kramer are right, the facts we point to and the principles we invoke and the authorities we cite are themselves system-of-difference-specific— that is, they are facts, principles and authorities *within* the very differential system whose judgments they are called on to warrant. Acts of validation can always be performed, but they will be performed inside a form of life or practice that (a) floats free of any anchoring tether in some independent reality, and (b) is always in the process of altering itself in the very act of applying itself. Every successful attempt by a literary system of differences to maintain its key terms—epic, novel, lyric, drama—in the face of phenomena they did not predict will be at once the redefinition of those terms and the transformation (an entirely internal operation) of that system. Every time a category of law—breach of contract, third party beneficiary, viewpoint discrimination, proximate cause—is stretched to include fact situations hitherto unimagined, that category becomes something other than it was, although in its form it is still the effect of the system of differences (now changed) that is the law. And every time a redefinition or a stretching cannot be accomplished— it persuades no one, the opinion just won't write—the system of differences trembles under the weight of internal strain and is ripe for what Thomas Kuhn famously termed a paradigm shift. Meanwhile, judgments continue to be made, reasons are given, progress is declared, but in the end and in the beginning (the question of origins is rigorously excluded from this form of thought), the roadway we walk on is one we continually construct by discursive means—systems of difference—that at once precede us and become changed by the work we do within them.

Or so went the story a lot of us were telling ourselves and each other in the 1970s and 80s. What was and continues to be exciting about that story is its immodesty. It wants to extend itself to everything "from the entire fabric of the universe to the most trifling substructures thereof"

(Kramer 6). As one of its most devoted tellers, I saw versions of it in nearly everything I came upon, including in a cartoon that appeared in *The New Yorker*. In the first of its two panels, a batter turns around to inquire of the umpire (who hasn't said anything yet), "Well, what was it, a ball or a strike?" In the second panel the umpire, thought to be the legendary Bill Klem, barks, "Sonny, it ain't nothing till I call it." It was immediately clear to me that Klem was a deep thinker in the anti-foundationalist tradition who heard in the batter's question—"Well, what was it, a ball or a strike?"—the familiar set of foundationalist assumptions: events and objects in the world exist and have their own shape independently of any of the descriptions they may receive; descriptions, in turn, have the job of being true to facts already in place before they are hazarded: it was either a ball or a strike, and the umpire's responsibility was to report faithfully on whichever it (antecedently) was. When Klem answered, "Sonny, it ain't nothing till I call it," he was saying (1) you've got it wrong; rather than existing independently of my verbal declaration, the facts about this pitch (or any other) are brought into being by my verbal declaration; they are discourse-produced facts; (2) they are produced not just when anyone speaks, but when I, or someone else in my institutional position, speaks (a fan yelling "ball" or "strike" will have no efficacy whatsoever); (3) the very possibility of a spheroid thrown sixty feet being either a ball or strike depends on the in-place system of differences known as baseball, with its structure of binaries: ball/strike, batter/pitcher, safe/out, single/double, ground ball/fly ball, fast ball/curve ball, top of the inning/bottom of the inning, grounded out/forced out, bunt/hit, walk/intentional walk; and (4) while this structure can change if the descriptive/discursive rules change— if, for example, a new rule brings into existence the "designated hitter"— what will not change is the constitutive force of my words.

The most general lesson of the cartoon, or so I said when teaching it to my students, was the lesson Protagoras taught in his famous pronouncement, "Man is the measure of all things," by which he meant that whatever might be true about the world from some vantage point far removed from human ways of knowing, human ways of knowing mark both the limits and the horizons of what can be true or false for us as limited, time-bound beings; and, moreover, since human ways of knowing are discursive—always take the form of predications intelligible only within some system of differences ("strike three," "you're out")— knowledge for human beings is discourse-specific, infinitely revisable, and never full or complete. This is a very old idea—the entire history of rhetoric from the pre-Socratics to Foucault is its elaboration—and it is an idea I found everywhere I looked. George Herbert provided a concise lyrical instance of it in these lines from his great poem "The Flower": "We say amisse, / This or that is: / Thy word is all, if we could spell" (19–21). That is, from God's point of view everything we see as discrete is unified and given meaning by his omnipresence; but distant as we are from that overarching perspective, we can only make assertions (say that this or that is) that are true or false in relation to a perspective or system of differences that is irremediably partial. Not only do we say amiss, saying is itself amiss and a sign of the infirmity we labor under as fallen beings.

In the same century, Thomas Hobbes makes the same point without the theological nostalgia: "*True* and *False*, are attributes of Speech, not of Things. And where Speech is not, there is neither *Truth* nor *Falsehood*" (105). Pieces of the world do not come tagged with meaning and value, both of which can only be conferred by acts of speech. Truth does not constrain discourse but is an effect of discourse, and later in *Leviathan* Hobbes makes morality an effect of discourse when he defines it as an aspect and by-product of contract, of the artificial stipulation by two agents of an exchange value to which they are subsequently bound, not by an abstract and preexisting moral obligation, but by the words they have jointly spoken and agreed to:

> For where no Covenant hath preceded, there hath no Right been transferred, and every man has right to every thing; and consequently, no action can be Unjust. But when a Covenant is made, then to break it is *Unjust*; And the definition of INJUSTICE, is no other than *the not Performance of Covenant*. And whatsoever is not Unjust, is *Just*. (202)

In this incomparably brilliant account of our moral life, the very concepts that in a foundationalist picture underwrite and order our verbal transactions become available and constraining only as a result of our verbal transactions. You can only say "that is unjust" if justice and injustice have first been given conventional (as opposed to necessary or natural) definitions to which all the relevant parties subscribe. The question of whether or not these definitions correspond to notions of justice and injustice that would be approved by God or Universal Reason never arises for Hobbes (who points out later that everyone claims to be in harmony with the will of God or the dictates of Universal Reason), just as the question of whether the pitch was "really"—that is, in some realm of fact independent of any established human practice—a ball or a strike never arises for Bill Klem. (The point would hold even in the age of "instant replay," for instant replay does not replace the institutionally binding judgment of the umpire with a judgment more objective; it merely provides a prosthetic aid to the institutionally embedded arbiter who must still make do with the resources and powers given to him by the game he at once plays and presides over.)

Bill Klem, George Herbert, Thomas Hobbes, my host's sister, Ferdinand de Saussure, my boyhood experience of an intersection in Providence, Rhode Island—it was out of these bits and pieces that I was fashioning the arguments Gary Olson and Hillis Miller discuss, and in the later decades of the century I added to this contingently assembled collection of touchstones the pronouncements of some of our most prominent and controversial thinkers: Nelson Goodman when he says, "If I ask about the world, you can offer to tell me how it is under one or more frames of reference; but if I insist that you tell me how it is apart from all frames," there is nothing you can say because in our human condition all we have are "ways of describing" (2–3); Thomas Kuhn when he says that since "a paradigm is prerequisite to perception itself" and all descriptive vocabularies are paradigm-specific, our inquiries always "presuppose a world already perceptually and conceptually subdivided in a certain way" (113, 129); Fredric Jameson when he says that history is "inaccessible to us except in textual form" (35); and J.L. Austin when he says, serially in a dazzling five pages, that (1) "reference depends on knowledge at the time of utterance"; (2) "it is essential to realize that 'true' and 'false,' like 'free' and 'unfree,' do not stand for anything simple at all, but only for a general dimension of being a right or proper thing to say as opposed to a wrong thing, in these circumstances, to this audience, for these purposes and with these intentions"; and (3) truth and falsity are "not names for relations, qualities, or what not, but for a dimension of assessment" (143–44, 148). Each of these remakes and extends the Hobbesian point, which is remade in almost the same language by Richard Rorty when he says, again in rapid succession, (1) "where there are no sentences there is no truth"; (2) "the world is out there, but descriptions of the world are not" and "only descriptions of the world can be true or false"; (3) "the world does not speak; only we do"; and (4) "since truth is a property of sentences, since sentences are dependent for their existence upon vocabularies, and since vocabularies are made by human beings, so are truths" (5–6, 21).

When you see these rather dramatic assertions lined up together, it is easy to understand why the argument they collectively make has been so fiercely resisted. If truth varies with the dimension of assessment currently in place or with the way of describing that happens to be in fashion or with the paradigm that mainstream researchers have internalized or with the vocabulary you happen to be using (all of these formulations are pretty much equivalent), then there is no hope of getting at what is *really*—apart from any dimension of assessment, way of describing, paradigm, or vocabulary—true, and in the words of Israel Scheffler, "Independent and public controls are no more, communication has failed, the common universe of things is a delusion, reality itself is made . . . rather than discovered" (19). For Scheffler, merely to enumerate these implications of the anti-foundationalist argument is sufficient to discredit it: if this is what anti-foundationalism leads you to, who would be so foolish as to affirm it?

Well, one answer I would have given to that question is John Milton; for in the years when I was hearing and responding to Scheffler-like objections, I was also elaborating a reading of *Paradise Lost* that had Milton dramatizing the very same issues I was trying to work through in my theoretical writings. (Or did it just seem that way to me? Was my reading of the poetry generated by my theoretical musings? Was it the other way around? Who can tell?) A key moment in that reading occurs in Book VI when Satan and the Archangel Michael square off in single combat and, in a ritual preliminary gesture, hurl insults at one another. Michael goes first and blames Satan for everything that has happened: "Author of evil, unknown till thy revolt" (262). Satan replies with a counter-declaration that marks him as the first postmodernist philosopher: "The strife which thou call'st evil . . . we style / The strife of glory" (289–90). That is, in our story, the story we both tell and live within, we are freedom fighters, an outnumbered but dedicated band determined to throw off the shackles of an imposed tyranny even though the tyrant occupies the rhetorical high ground (he calls himself God) and boasts superior weaponry. Of course, Michael has his own story, one of fidelity to an all-powerful and benevolent deity who, as the source of all value and meaning, breathes inspiriting life into creatures who are incapable of breaking free of him and who run the risk of losing their very beings by making the vain attempt: "Who can impair thee, mighty King . . . ? / Who seeks / To lessen thee, against his purpose serves / To manifest the more thy might" (VII, 608, 613–15).

So much is clear, but what is not clear, and could not be clear according to Milton, is which of the two stories is really, as opposed to perspectivally or narratively, true. Another archangel, Raphael, poses the crucial question when he asks "to convince the proud what Signs avail?" (VI, 789). What fact, or event, or outcome would be sufficiently weighty and perspicuous to persuade the rebels that they were in the wrong? The answer is contained in the scorn with which Raphael puts the question. Nothing would be sufficient (necessarily) to persuade them, for whatever came their way they could with a little interpretive effort or without any effort at all contrive to see it as evidence of the presuppositions that impel them. Do they experience pain for the first time? It merely gives them something to disdain and "contemn," something that proves rather than undercuts their heroism (VI, 432). Do they provoke God to send his terrible chariot against them? Another indication of how seriously they are taken by the enemy and a spur to fighting on. Are they thrown out of Heaven and into the burning lake of Hell? Just another opportunity to be inventive (they build a great castle in seconds) and to reassess their situation in anticipation of the next assault (which, in the poem's fable, is successful).

What makes Milton's treatment of his characters' epistemological situation so contemporary, and so much grist for my theoretical mill, is that it extends to the loyal angels as well, for they too occupy a position that seems invulnerable to counter-evidence from the outside. They serve, as William Empson first pointed out, a deity who sends them on unnecessary errands in order to deprive them of pleasures they would otherwise enjoy, who gives them assignments (drive the rebels out) he knows them unable to perform, who demands that they prepare themselves for efforts that will never be needed, who exposes them to ridicule and humiliation (when they are overwhelmed by hill-sized pies thrown at them by the enemy), and who requires of them endless hymns of praise and adoration. No wonder, says Empson, that his Chinese students found confirmation of the perversity of the English in the perverse God they worshiped. It would seem that Raphael's question could be turned on himself: "To convince the loyalists, what Signs avail?" The answer, again, is none. No matter what happens, no matter how many times legitimate expectations are disappointed, no matter how inscrutable the pronouncements and the will of him they serve, no matter how much evidence piles up that could be read as supporting the rebel "styling" of the epic strife, they persist.

Why? Or in Schefflerian terms, in the absence of independent and public controls and of a universe the details of which are commonly agreed to, how does one go on? Raphael gives the answer in terms that reaffirm the story he believes in but that also affirm the postmodern lesson

that, as far as we can know, the story is underwritten by nothing firmer or
more "objective" (independent) than the inner conviction of those who
live it out:

> Myself and all th' Angelic Host that stand
> In sight of God enthron'd, our happy state
> Hold, as you yours, while our obedience holds;
> On other surety none. (V, 535–38)

That is to say, the world we live in—with God at its center and the
obligations, opportunities, meanings, and facts entailed by his centrality—exists and persists ("holds") as long as we believe in it. No brute data
available and perspicuous apart from our belief provides independent
warrant for that belief. No score card or annual report objectively
confirms that we are on the right track. No event that occurs or word that
is spoken (even if spoken by God) bears an inescapable meaning that
imprints itself unmistakably on the understanding of all parties. Everything—the values we affirm, the courses of action we find compelling, the
truths we pledge allegiance to—acquires and retains shape and significance only through the exertion of a will that is radically free to change
the objects of its devotion: "Freely we serve, / Because we freely love, as
in our will / To love or not" (538–40). And, moreover, whatever you
love—God, truth, the American way, baseball, poetry, opera, mathemat-
ics, capitalism, the Internet—is not *obviously* lovable; there will always
be those who do not love it, and to those you can say many things—tell
your story, recite your creed, celebrate wonders, declaim poems, perform
arias—but you can never say the thing (because there is no such thing)
that is in and of itself irresistible, conclusive and definitive, now,
tomorrow, always.

The life one lives under this vision is marked by provisionality and
improvisation. Like the Abraham of *Hebrews* XI, you act on the basis of
a faith that is its own foundation ("On other surety none"): "By faith
Abraham, when he was called . . . obeyed; and he went out, not knowing
whither he went." And when that faith is met by what seems counter-
evidence—your people wander in the desert for forty years and later
endure a Babylonian captivity, the monarchy is restored in 1660, the
forces of the Third Reich occupy France and much else of Western
Europe, six million die in gas chambers—you either recharacterize that
evidence so that, despite appearances, it becomes a reason for persisting,
or you respond to it by abandoning your faith for another, itself no more

securely anchored in public and independent controls, no more *sure*, than the faith you now regard as error. In short, you act exactly as Kuhn says you act when you mount experiments on the basis of paradigmatic assumptions that create rather than discover the facts they stipulate to; you live for a while in the world delivered by that paradigm, by that faith, the world of phlogiston or ether or "planets and pendulums, condensers and compound ores," and then, for reasons and causes that can be analyzed after the fact but that are not predictable or the result of design, the paradigm changes, and researchers practice their trade in what is, for all intents and purposes, a "different world" (128, 150), just as Satan thinks himself into a different world when in an instant of cosmic resentment (he reads God's exaltation of the Son as an affront to his dignity), he exchanges a paradigm of obedience for a paradigm of revolution, and in that moment imagines into being a capricious father, an unfairly favored younger son, and countless sycophantic angels who witness an injustice but do not protest it.

The correspondences between the Kuhnian and the Miltonic visions are many (and we could add to them the Rortian vision with its vocabularies that elaborate and reelaborate worlds teeming with facts, distinctions, judgments of better or worse, all in place and operating without benefit of a metaphysical or ontological tether), and extend to Kuhn's refusal to provide a formula for producing the changes and revolutions science brings in its wake, a refusal he makes in theological terms: "The transfer of allegiance from paradigm to paradigm [from faith to faith] is a conversion experience that cannot be forced"; the conversion experience "remains, therefore, at the heart of the revolutionary process"; each party "must try, by persuasion, to convert the other" (151, 204, 198). And since the success of persuasion will always be contingent—Satan persuaded many angels, but not Abdiel—you can never tell how things will come out: "The competition between paradigms is not the sort of battle that can be resolved by proofs" (no more than Michael could prove to Satan that his actions were evil). "There is no neutral algorithm for theory-choice, no systematic decision procedure which, properly applied, must lead each individual in the group to the same decision" (148, 200).

As I shuttled back and forth between the two poles of my academic life, Renaissance poetry and twentieth-century interpretive theory, I more and more came to see them as one thing. To be sure, there was the difference that in the writings of Kuhn and Rorty and Austin there was little mention of God (although Derrida is always at least flirting with theology), but that was finally not that much of a difference, since in Milton's work (or Herbert's or Donne's) the fact of God does not help those who believe in him when they are confronted with a moral or political decision and must decide what to do. They know that they must identify and obey God's will, but with no direct access to that will, they must make do with mediations and fashion lives hazarded on an act of faith that will not be redeemed or proven in this world; they must say truths that are rooted in a hope the flowering of which they will not see in this life. ("Faith is the substance of things hoped for, the evidence of things not seen.") This, I believe, is the final and most important link between the poetry I have been teaching and the theoretical or anti-theoretical argument I have been refining all these years: although both concern themselves with very large questions to which they give very large answers, those answers are too large to provide any guidance once one moves away from the rarified precincts of their general formulation and descends (if that is the right word, and it may not be) to particulars. Just as a Miltonic hero (Abdiel, Samson, Adam) cannot translate a conviction of God's power and benevolence into a recipe for action because the paths of action are ambiguously marked in ways not resolved by that general conviction, so is the conviction either that there are or that there are not independent grounds for our conclusions of no help in reaching them. Whatever the resources we make use of when we are called upon to decide and to act, they will not be the resources of either foundationalism or anti-foundationalism, names of positions we might affirm, but not of programs we might execute. Long after leaving Providence, Rhode Island, I am still stopped at that intersection, thinking about what to do next.

University of Illinois
Chicago, Illinois

Introduction

My first introduction to Stanley Fish was as a student in a Milton seminar. The instructor was an unusually animated and entertaining performer who would race around the room reading passages from *Paradise Lost* in viva voce and who insisted that we imagine the epic as the prototype of modern superhero comic books. We were to envision Satan as a caped archenemy, springing from here to there with fiendish energy, much like one of Spiderman's indefatigable foes. Needless to say, this instructor did much to make Milton come alive, even for the most jaded among us. At the opening of class one day, he burst into the seminar room brandishing a copy of Fish's *Surprised by Sin*. The book had begun to cause a furor not only among Miltonists but among many in English studies, and our instructor had just finished reading it. Even though we were accustomed to his frenetic teaching style, nothing could have prepared us for the vociferous agitation he unleashed on us that day. Slamming the book down on the seminar table, his bald head glowing red, he sputtered uncontrollably as he spit out his words: "This book is an abomination! This is *not* how you read Milton, and it's *not* how you do literary criticism! Don't waste your time and money on such drivel!" (As might be expected, we all immediately and surreptitiously ordered our own copies of this forbidden fruit to discover what magic resided there.) Throughout the remainder of the semester, our instructor would signify an errant reading of a passage from Milton by snarling, "That sounds Fishy to me!" Ever since that day, Fish's works have become required reading for me.

As it turned out, this Miltonist's vehement reaction to Fish's book was characteristic, if somewhat overplayed, of how many readers re-

1

ceived this groundbreaking work of criticism. And the controversy did not end there; from that time onward, Fish's work has always polarized readers. People such as Geoffrey Galt Harpham can credit Fish with being "one of the very best essayists in any field," saying that one essay in particular ("Consequences") demonstrates "dazzling intelligence," while such critics as Valentine Cunningham can declare that Fish is "crass" and that his Clarendon Lectures at Oxford were "intellectually sullying" and "morally disgusting."[1] His work seems to elicit either admiration or disdain—rarely anything in between. There simply is no such thing as a tepid response to Fish's work.

Despite the monumental influence that Fish has exerted on the study of seventeenth-century poetry and prose, his most widely read works—and some would say his most important—are his nonliterary writings. *Justifying Belief* examines some of Fish's important nonliterary work. It begins with an examination of his perspective on English studies as a discipline, especially as presented in *Professional Correctness: Literary Studies and Political Change*. Fish takes issue with those who hope to transform literary studies so that it is more directly connected with contemporary political issues and struggles such as sexism, racism, and homophobia. He insists that so long as literary critics operate *as* academics within the constraints and forums of the discipline, they will necessarily reach only a relatively small number of people and thus will exert little or no political influence. He contends further that if they depart from the usual modes of expression, methodologies, and forums of the discipline and thereby discover some degree of political effectivity outside of the academy, they will no longer be operating as literary critics: they will be operating as something *other* than literary critics. This argument is a direct response to the new historicists, to cultural studies advocates, and to those who dream that it is possible to resurrect the notion of the public intellectual: someone that the public consistently turns to for insight on any number of subjects, not only on issues deriving from his or her academic area but on a wide range of subjects relevant to a broad audience. Fish concludes that despite the good intentions of these socially conscious academics, such hopes are simply unrealizable.

A substantial number of Fish's works cluster around a single argument: that general principles do not and cannot inform specific practice. Chapter 2 focuses on this argument, first by examining his contention that theory has no consequence for the practice of literary criticism and then by looking at that same argument as it applies to the teaching of composition. He contends that while the objective of most theories is to elucidate, inform, or improve practice, a theory will not substantively affect the practice it considers—literary criticism, the teaching of composition, or any other practice. The chapter then looks at how Fish has broadened his anti-theory argument to encompass any appeal to general principle. To make this case, he addresses issues arising from contemporary debates about liberal political philosophy, First Amendment rights, affirmative action policies, and multiculturalism. He argues that central to liberal political philosophy is the notion that a just society is based on such principles as "fairness," principles that supposedly exist in the abstract, independent of any specific situation or context. He concludes that although such abstractions are thought to be capable of being defined in ways that allow them to remain free from partisan agendas and, thus, are thought to be capable of serving as the foundation of legal and political policies that favor no one person or group in particular but that respect all people and groups in general, such efforts are doomed to fail.

What unites Fish's interventions in so many disparate areas of inquiry is his belief in the centrality of rhetoric. Whether he is discussing how disciplines conduct their work, how political positions triumph, or how practice always derives from specific situations despite the grandiose theories employed to justify them, he consistently turns to the specific local, contingent context—to the rhetorical situation at play—to explain how something works. A primary task of rhetoric is to justify our beliefs. For Fish, beliefs are constitutive of consciousness; that is, in many ways we are what we believe. People "understand" or are "persuaded" by a position or belief because it fits into the structure of beliefs already in play, not because they have been swayed by the "reasonableness" of someone's argument; they then pursue the available means of support to justify that belief rhetorically, both to themselves and to others. For the liberal rationalist, the mind operates independent of any particular belief, coolly and rationally assessing contending beliefs to determine which ones make sense; for Fish, beliefs are the content of rationality, in the sense that rationality arises from beliefs and not the other way around. We justify a belief, then, by turning to the structure of beliefs from which the belief derives its intelligibility and within which it is coherent, and we then seek to express that intelligibility and coherence rhetorically, establishing a case for the belief. This strong relationship between rhetoric and belief is the intellectual foundation of much of Fish's work.

Chapters 4 and 5 are interviews with Fish about his nonliterary work. The first was conducted in 1991, the second in 2000. In them, Fish explores and clarifies many of the positions he has taken over the years, and he reaffirms his conviction that rhetoric is the "necessary center." In addition, he describes his own writing process and how it has changed over the years. While Fish has certainly made an indelible mark on intellectual history with his nonliterary work, he comments in the most recent interview that he is especially proud of his work as a literary critic. He sees his lasting legacy as his contribution to English studies: the numerous essays and books on such authors as Milton, Herbert, Donne, Marvell, Jonson, Burton, and Bacon—many of which are "still doing work in their fields." In the Afterword to *Justifying Belief*, J. Hillis Miller reflects on Fish's work and its contribution to contemporary understandings of the interrelationships among rhetoric, epistemology, and belief. The book ends with a comprehensive bibliography of Fish's works.

What impresses me most about Fish's work is the intellectual integrity with which he tackles whatever issue is in question. Almost a decade ago, I served as Fish's host when he came to my institution to stage the first in a series of debates with Dinesh D'Souza about "political correctness" and affirmative action. These debates were held at universities across the country and were advertised as the academic equivalent of boxing's heavyweight title matches. In fact, I remember delivering Fish to the crowded Dean's office prior to the evening's event and being mortified that the university's president then proceeded to advise the two contenders "not to hold back any punches" because the crowd expected a "knockout blow." The debate took place in a large auditorium and, like a title match, was held before a standing-room-only crowd—in this case, well over five hundred spectators. I'm certain that no one went away disappointed that night, but what I discovered to my dismay was that my own impression of the debate—that is, in the parlance used at the time, my notion of "who won"—was entirely different from that of many other spectators. D'Souza, prepped and groomed by the American Enterprise Institute, would hurl neatly polished sound bites, tidy one-liners, and pithy anecdotes. He'd mention the English major who managed to graduate having read Toni Morrison but not Shakespeare, and the law school applicant with stunningly impressive academic credentials who was denied admission in place of a less-qualified minority applicant. Fish, in contrast, took pains to analyze the issues in their full complexity, "Oh, the literary canon? Let me tell you where we got the canon in the first place. . . ." He would then proceed to furnish a wonderfully detailed and nuanced account of canon formation. In my estimation, Fish's performance was far more substantive and intellectually compelling than D'Souza's, precisely because Fish took no shortcuts, hurled no one-liners, employed no sound bites. He approached intellectual issues (as he customarily does) with an acknowledgment of and a faithfulness to their full complexity. In an age ablur with streaming video and rapid sound bites, however, a D'Souza is much more likely to capture the imagination—that is, entertain—than someone who is committed to fully interrogating a subject. What had struck me and some of my colleagues as substantive, compelling and, thus, as "winning" struck others as "not as entertaining" and, thus, as "losing."[2] Regardless of who won any debate, Fish brings this same intellectual integrity to everything he writes. He takes no shortcuts, and he typically anticipates the major objections to his line of reasoning, provides a faithful rendering of those objections, and then proceeds to explain why they are misguided. It's no wonder, then, that he can be called "one of the very best essayists in any field."

After the debate, Fish and D'Souza sat at separate tables in the lobby autographing copies of their books. As the crowd thinned, I noticed a disheveled, rather sinister looking man lurking in a corner. When Fish completed his book signing, he strode over to wait with me; we were to have a cocktail with D'Souza. The sinister character stepped out of the shadows and walked straight up to Fish. "It's you Jews who are responsible for the shape this country's in," he exclaimed threateningly. "You own the media and. . . ." Fearing that this person represented a clear danger to Fish, I stepped between them and informed the stranger that we had no time to converse, as we were leaving for an appointment. Always prepared to debate anyone—perhaps even the devil himself—Fish gently pushed me aside and exclaimed, "You're right! But you're forgetting something. . . ." And he proceeded to engage this character in a lively discussion. I have no idea if the stranger really did represent a threat, or if Fish was even aware that this person seemed more interested in confrontation than intellectual conversation; the salient fact is that Stanley Fish has never turned down a good (verbal) fight; it seems to be what he lives for. As he says in the interview in chapter 5, "There are a lot of people out there making mistakes, and I'm just going to tell them that they're making mistakes."

I would like to thank a number of people who helped make this project possible. Allison Brimmer, Tammy Evans, and Merry Perry worked diligently to compile, track down, and verify every entry in the book's bibliography of Fish's works—a truly gargantuan task. Colleen Connolly, Deepa Sitaraman, and Karen Samuels provided indispensable research assistance. Joyce Karpay proofread the manuscript with an eagle's eye. Priscilla Ross prodded me to undertake this project and was ever on my mind as it progressed. And Lynn Worsham sustained me with her wit and penetrating intelligence and also served as my first reader and sharpest critic. I would also like to thank both Stanley Fish and J. Hillis Miller, not only for their contributions to this project, but for their generous support over the years.

Chapter 1

Public Intellectuals and the Discipline of English Studies

> Changing the mode of literary analysis or changing the object of literary analysis or changing the name of literary analysis will not change the material effectiveness of literary analysis and make it into an instrument of political action. That kind of change, if it is ever to occur, will require wholesale *structural* changes of which literary analysts might take advantage, but which they could never initiate.
>
> —Stanley Fish

> The conservatism of intellectual and academic institutions is more powerful than the imagination of those who predict their evolution.
>
> —Stanley Fish

Stanley Fish has always, almost from the beginning of his career, had much to say about the "profession," about the internal workings of English studies—its objectives, its methodologies, even how it might be renamed given the massive changes the discipline has undergone over the last quarter of a century. His most cogent and provocative statement has been a small book, *Professional Correctness: Literary Studies and Political Change,* which is a revision of the Clarendon Lectures, a prestigious invitational lecture series sponsored each year by Oxford University. He presented the lectures in the Spring of 1993, but he conceived the project—its arguments, its shape, its general thrust—at the end of 1990 when he conducted a workshop at the Folger Library in Washington, DC. As with so much that Fish has published, this book prompted considerable antipathy from a fair number of readers. He was accused of being *against* historical work in literary studies, *against* political work in English studies, *against* cultural studies, *against* interdisciplinary work in general. Not only does a close reading of *Professional Correctness* demonstrate that such charges are baseless, Fish himself anticipates all of these allegations and addresses them, both in the Preface and in the Appendix of the book. Nevertheless, critics, especially those with progressive orientations, continue to characterize this work as a conservative or even reactionary diatribe against attempts to make English studies more politically effective in the world outside of the academy.

The Distinctiveness of Literary Studies

The main thesis of the lectures is itself rather simple and straightforward: Fish argues that despite the claims of those who are attempting to transform literary studies so that it is more deeply and directly connected with contemporary political issues and struggles—sexism, racism, homophobia, terrorism, and so on—when literary critics are operating *as* academics within the constraints and forums of the discipline, they will necessarily be reaching only a relatively small number of people (their colleagues in the discipline) and thus will have little or no political effectiveness; conversely, if they depart from the usual modes of expression, methodologies, and forums of the discipline and thereby discover some degree of political effectivity outside of the academy, they will no longer be operating as literary critics: they will be operating as something *other* than literary critics. Now, he hastens to add that we may very well judge this new way of operating to be valuable—in fact, we may even value it more than we value a work of criticism—but the fact remains that such political work is *not* literary criticism; it is something different. What's more, this new work is not ipso facto superior or inferior to a work of criticism; it, again, is simply different.

This argument rests on a strong notion of what it means to be a "specialist." As Fish points out, a literary critic is a particular kind of specialist, and all specialists are defined by the specific traditions, histories, techniques, vocabularies, and methods of inquiry of their specializations. In fact, it is exactly this unique set of traditions, histories, techniques, vocabularies, and methods of inquiry that allows them to be defined as specialists in a particular endeavor in the first place. As a field, literary criticism—despite the competing practices, assumptions, or epistemological orientations of its individual practitioners—is constituted by certain shared objectives and ways of defining its practice over and against the practices of other academic disciplines. That is, it exhibits a unique culture and way of asserting its distinctiveness.

The issue of "distinctiveness" is central to Fish's argument. He takes what in effect is a Derridian stance in pointing out that any given thing is defined in contrast to all the things that it is not. Literary criticism is what it is because it is *not* sociology or history or critical legal studies, and so on—although at times it may borrow from these and other disciplines. That is, we understand a discipline to be what it is because it can successfully present itself to its own members and to the external world as performing some specific set of tasks that only it can accomplish or that other disciplines are not as qualified to perform. Fish is careful to caution that he should not be read as adopting an essentialist notion of disciplinarity or of the discipline of literary studies. He acknowledges that disciplinary boundaries are always in flux, always being renegotiated: "Negotiations on the borders go on continually, and at times border skirmishes can turn into large-scale territorial disputes in which the right of an enterprise to the space it has long occupied is hotly contested" (19). Despite these battles, however, a discipline will nonetheless remain coherent precisely because when all is said and done it still performs a unique set of specific tasks.

Once a discipline can present itself to the world as being uniquely qualified to perform a certain set of tasks—explicating poems, say—it will achieve, says Fish, autonomy as a discipline; it will stand on its own as an intellectual area independent of others. According to Fish, while the boundaries of literary criticism have waxed and waned over time, the core project has remained constant: to determine what works of literature "mean." The paradigmatic question of literary criticism, then, is, "What does this poem (or novel or play) *mean*?" (34). Thus, the distinctiveness of the activity we call "literary criticism" derives from the dialectical relationship between a work deemed (in advance) "literary" and the critic's setting out to read (interpret) that work *as* a piece of literature. A poem is categorized as a poem and not a theological sermon or political tract because it exhibits a certain linguistic and semantic density, and the critic approaches the poem with a cognizance of this density. In fact, says Fish, "Linguistic and semantic density is not something poems announce, but something that readers actualize by paying to texts labelled poetic a kind of attention they would not pay to texts not so labelled" (13). What ensues in the critical act, then, is an act of interpretation.

For Fish, "interpretation" applies to all participants in the critical act: the readers of the poem as well as its author. The readers apply a clearly defined set of interpretive strategies to the poem, and these strategies are so constitutive of the act that they "fill the consciousness" of the enterprise's members, thereby making the use of these strategies less a matter of free choice ("I choose to employ these strategies and not others") than of being swept into an activity that has a character and operating assumptions all its own. Similarly, the poet is a co-interpreter who works within the constraints of a well-established field (producing poems, in this example) and who draws on a distinct set of available strategies in attempting to match his or her intentions to those of the audience. That is, the relationship between authors and their readers is one in which all participants are "engaged in the mutual performance of a single task," and they are "at once constrained and enabled by the same history that burdens and energizes" their respective efforts (14). By "constrained and enabled," he means that the tradition and conventions of literary criticism make available the guiding assumptions and interpretive strategies that a critic will—or, more accurately, must—employ when producing a reading; the critic is in the grasp, if you will, of a particular way of understanding and approaching the critical act. At the same time, this very set of guiding assumptions and interpretive strategies is what authorizes or makes possible the critical act in the first place.

Because critics are in the grasp of a particular way of understanding and approaching the critical act, they in effect begin in the middle of a process that has already begun:

> They go about their business not in order to discover its point, but already in possession of and possessed by its point. They ask questions and give answers—not, however, any old questions and answers, but questions and answers of the kind they know in advance to be relevant. In a sense they could not even ask the questions if they did not already know the answers to questions deeper than the ones they are explicitly asking. (15)

In other words, the critic approaches a text guided—in effect, controlled—by a prior understanding not only of what the act of literary interpretation entails but what a work of literature is in the first place, and this prior understanding restricts the critic's interpretive behavior (what kinds of questions and strategies are appropriate and what are not) at the same time that it provides a clear way of proceeding.

The critic produces a reading of a literary work within and because of this unique and specialized context. In fact, it is the very fact of being located within this specific praxis that marks its participants (fellow critics) as particular kinds of specialists who are jointly operating within a common field and by ways that are immediately intelligible to one another. Despite the micro-level differences that separate the activities of one kind of critic from another—a deconstructionist from a Marxist, say—it is the larger set of common prior understandings about praxis that establish all critics as participants in a common endeavor, an endeavor that in general is clearly different from other intellectual endeavors. That is, we recognize the practice of literary criticism as a discrete endeavor because we can contrast it with other intellectual endeavors and immediately ascertain that it is distinct from them. As Fish says, it is a "requirement for the respectability of an enterprise that it be, or at least be able to present itself as, *distinctive*" (17). What's more, the activity of literary criticism is primarily an "academic" endeavor: it takes place mostly in academic settings, is pursued by people who take a specialized course of training to undertake the activity, and is judged according to standards established by the "academic guild." It is this very process of professionalization that serves to ensure that the discipline maintains its ever-important distinctiveness.

To say that all critics operate from a larger set of common prior understandings about their praxis is not to suggest that this praxis is immutable, frozen in one unchangeable form. Fish points out that, as with any profession, literary criticism is constantly undergoing internal scrutiny as new people enter the field and begin to question the operating assumptions and strategies that are in place when they arrive. Such scrutiny may and often will lead to debates within the field about how the business of the discipline should be conducted, and it may even lead to proposed changes in the established praxis. This is a common and healthy process evident in any disciplinary area; however, no matter how much the discipline is confronted with proposed operational changes or new or unassimilated material (the field should now pay attention to these as of yet unexplored areas), it will not abandon what Fish calls its "immanent intelligibility," its internal coherence as a field of study distinct from all other fields. In fact, confronted by such challenges, it is most likely to reassert its immanent intelligibility, either by strengthening its previously established disciplinary borders or by extending those borders to include the new concerns. Either way, the discipline will appeal to its own coherence as a distinct endeavor, arguing either that the changes are inappropriate because they threaten its distinctiveness or that they are appropriate because they in fact fall within the purview of its distinct mission and way of operating. Thus, at any given moment the discipline will be undergoing self-scrutiny of one sort or another, and it will measure all challenges against how those challenges will affect its disciplinary distinctiveness, its immanent intelligibility.

Of course, it is entirely possible that over time the members of a discipline can forget or underestimate or not comprehend the importance of the field's immanent intelligibility to its continued existence and thus allow its borders to expand so immeasurably that the discipline would then lose its distinct shape; that is, it is possible for a discipline to lose its distinctiveness and thus no longer be able to claim that it performs tasks useful to anyone beyond its own borders. This is precisely the scenario that Fish worries may be happening to English studies as it embraces new historicism and cultural studies. If the discipline becomes so inclusive that it no longer can clearly articulate "what we do around here," it is in danger of becoming a nondiscipline:

> Today, of course, there is no end of argument about the precise parameters of "what we do around here"; but those who engage in the argument push against a sense of boundaries strongly (some would say too strongly) in place. The fact that there are disputes about literary studies is less significant than the fact that the disputes are about something assumed to possess its own rationale and therefore to have achieved "immanent intelligibility." It is an achievement, however, that brings with it a considerable cost; for if, from the vantage-point of a shared expertise, we can now intelligibly say "That's not the kind of thing we do around here," we are without defence when someone turns around and says to us, "Your specialized skills have no claim on our attention, for that's not the kind of thing *we* do around *here*." (29–30)

That is, it is no surprise that literary studies, like any other discipline, engages in continual self-reflection; the relevant fact is that the general parameters of the field and its assumed rationale have remained unquestioned, and thus its distinctiveness is in place. The true danger is in expanding those borders to such a degree that someone—a university's administration, say—can justifiably announce that the kind of activity that we claim to specialize in is not of any use to the institution. In such a scenario, one can easily imagine English studies going the way of classics in the university curricula.

New Historicism and its Discontents

> I set out to consider the claims and hopes of those who believe that literary criticism can be made to engage directly and effectively with the project of restructuring the whole of modern society.
> —Stanley Fish

> The vocabularies of disciplines are not external to their objects, but constitutive of them. Discard them in favour of the vocabulary of another discipline, and you will lose the object that only they call into being.
> —Stanley Fish

It is certainly true, says Fish, that in past centuries the craft of *writing* a piece of literature was much more closely linked to the political life of the culture. Queen Elizabeth and James I produced their own literature, and many of the canonized authors whose work we cherish today were underwritten or supported by powerful patrons in the governments of their times. As a result, many of these authors enjoyed a kind of entrée to the corridors of power that would be quite impossible—or at least unlikely—today. Thus, prior to our own age, the literary and political were much more closely aligned. A renowned poet in the sixteenth or seventeenth century, say, might very well produce a poem that he hoped would influence a certain political outcome, and he might even have a reasonable expectation, given who his patrons happened to be in relation to the issue that he was trying to influence, of exerting some political pressure.[1] Nevertheless, even though certain authors in the sixteenth and seventeenth centuries could also act in the political arena, they did so by making use of their *literary* skills: by writing poems or other literary works. That is, they employed their distinctly *literary* competence to effect political ends. Today, the relationship between the literary and the political is, for all intents and purposes, nonexistent:

What distinguishes them from us is that they could contemplate
incorporating that literary intention into a political one by, say,
writing a poem intended to influence military or diplomatic policy.
They would then be putting to political effect a competence that
was not, in and of itself, political at all. In short, they could
reasonably intervene in political matters by exercising literary
skills. (33)

One effect of the triumph of liberal political philosophy is that no longer
can an author expect to incorporate a literary intention into a political one.
Literary works are generally seen as "the effusions of essentially free
minds," and while that means that the state can no longer regulate their
production, it also means that they have lost their strong connection to
political efficacy (36).

Notice that this discussion concerns *producers*, not *analysts* of
literature; it would be exceedingly difficult to make the case that literary
critics *ever* had political effectivity. The discipline of literary studies—
the profession devoted to asking, "What does this poem mean?—is a little
over a century old, and in that time it has carved out a distinctive niche for
itself and has thus been able to successfully justify its existence. While
the connection between the literary and the political has remained severed
for all of that time, some critics are now attempting to reconnect literary
studies to political action. Fish is particularly concerned about the claims
of the new historicists. He cites pleas that we begin to conceive of our
work as more than the "merely literary" and that literary studies
become a politically emancipatory endeavor. Some new historicists
claim that critical work can have an impact on the larger culture
beyond our classrooms and scholarly forums when we develop strategies of subversive reading that challenge or overturn conventional
thought and received opinion. Still others contend that we can and
should "stretch" and "violate" the rules of how literary analysis gets
done.

In response to these claims, Fish asserts that the rules of how a
discipline operates are always subject to change, but not just any change;
a change will derive from the discipline's own sense of mission, immanent intelligibility, and sense of appropriateness. A particular change
may very well catch on, thereby producing a new understanding of how
something is done; but this new way of doing things will always emanate
from and reflect the discipline's specific praxis, its distinctive contribution to intellectual work. And while critics can certainly produce readings

that subvert or call into question *doxa* or received opinion or conventional thought, they do not simply produce a reading because it is politically expedient (unless, of course they are propagandists instead of literary critics); rather, they are first persuaded by a given reading, captured by the reading's perspicuity and cogency. That is, one "doesn't 'choose' one's readings; one is *persuaded* to them, and one is persuaded to them not by calculating their political effects, but by coming up with answers to questions that are constitutive of the present practice of producing readings" (48). Even when one sets out to produce a new or subversive or revolutionary reading of a literary work, such a reading will necessarily occur "*within* and not in opposition to the normal routines of the discipline's business, routines that are at once open, in that they accommodate themselves to novelty, and closed, in that the aftermath of accommodation is a reconfiguration and not an elimination of a disciplinary boundary" (48–49). Hence, such readings could hardly be called "oppositional" in any meaningful sense because the very act of conceiving them will necessarily depend on conventional ways of thinking; indeed, they depend on the very *authority* of those conventional ways of thinking. In other words, for a reading of a literary work to count as legitimate (as a critical reading and not as something else), it has to be recognizable to other critics as "the kind of thing we do around here," even if individuals would object to the specific content or conclusions of the reading. The questions it poses and the answers it posits must be recognizably literary, deriving from the specific traditions, histories, techniques, vocabularies, and methods of inquiry conventional to the practice of literary criticism.

What confuses many critics who call for literary studies to become more politically effective is that they conflate two senses of *political*. When critics produce a reading of a literary work, they will undoubtedly be engaging in politics, but only in a weak sense. That is, they will be participating in the micro-politics of their subdiscipline—Shakespeare studies, say—in that any given reading will be contested by some colleagues and supported by others, or its particular methodological spin will be rejected by some and affirmed by others. Fish maintains that it is necessary to distinguish this general sense of the political (the sense in which on a certain level everything is contestable and therefore political) from the more substantive and consequential understanding of the political: the realm in which elections are won and lost, policies adopted or rejected, programs instituted or eliminated. He observes that when critics produce new or revolutionary or subversive readings of literary works, they may well be participating in academic or disciplinary politics, but they are not engaging in the kind of consequential politics that will have effects in the world external to the academy—the very kind of politics that they hope and at times claim to influence. Fish insists repeatedly throughout *Professional Correctness* that despite the intention of the critic or the critic's particular theoretical orientation—new historicist, cultural materialist, or any other—the interpretation of literary works does not have (and is not likely to have in the future) any immediate connection to the kinds of issues and concerns that circulate in the larger world of politics.

To the chagrin of many new historicists and others who hope to transform literary studies, Fish's argument that literary analysis will not lead to effective political action is specific to *literary* work, not to academic work in general. The simple fact of being an academic and performing academic tasks does not preclude someone from influencing political decisions through his or her academic work. Certain law professors, for example, can count on at least the possibility of exerting such influence through their research and publications. In contrast, there are no routine and customary avenues by which literary scholarship can and does make its way to the centers of political power. As Fish says on more than one occasion, all strong connections between the literary and the political have long been broken and seem irreparable: "The moral is clear, and fatal both to the ambitions of the new historicists and to the fears of those who oppose them: no one cares very much about literary criticism outside the confines of its *professional* practice" (55).[2] And this would continue to be the case even if new historicists or others were able to change the internal workings of the discipline:

> Even when new historicists alter their interpretive practices so as to reflect the conviction that both the objects of their attention and the forms of that attention are deeply implicated in society-wide structures of power and legitimization, the analyses they produce will not constitute an intervention in those structures. . . . The return to literary criticism of political questions does not make literary criticism more political in any active sense. (55)

That is, because there are no longer any routine and customary avenues by which literary work can and does make its way to the centers of political power—and this has been the case, some would say, for at least two centuries—it is no longer part of the mindset of legislators or other politicians to seek counsel from producers of literature, much less from analysts of literature; so even if a great number of literary critics were to begin writing their scholarship with political issues and an audience of politicians in mind, no one but the usual consumers of literary criticism would be listening.[3]

Anticipating certain objections to this argument, Fish acknowledges that debates about multiculturalism and political correctness during the late 1980s and early 1990s thrust the humanities into the public's attention when conservative commentators launched vigorous and vocal attacks on the humanities, especially on English studies. As a consequence, certain academics who enjoyed more visibility than most, Fish included, briefly found themselves on television talk shows or in the op-ed pages of national newspapers defending this or that academic practice or theory against the inflammatory rhetoric of such adversaries as George Will. Most of the critics who attempted to perform in the public spotlight were unprepared for the kind of onslaughts they faced. As a result, the entire discipline was embattled and on the defensive, "forced to answer the charge that its most prominent members believed that words are meaningless, that values and standards are political impositions, that interpretation is entirely a matter of force and will, that no one's interpretation can be said to be wrong, that there is no rationale for deciding when one work is better than another. (I know of no influential theorists who believe any of these things.)" (63). While this scenario might at first glance seem to contradict the argument that the work of literary critics is of no interest to the public and that critics have no role to play in the public arena, Fish contends that these apparent exceptions actually *prove* his thesis. He points out that those critics who entered the public consciousness did so not by virtue of their own efforts but by virtue of the efforts of those who were seeking to turn them into "symbols of a threat they do not in fact pose." What's more, what outraged the commentators who were pillorying these critics was not their literary scholarship, their close analysis of texts; rather, it was the implications that such commentators drew (usually erroneously) from the critics' work. Thus, the cause of their momentary prominence was not the work they did *as* literary interpreters; they were temporarily prominent solely on the basis of their symbolic value in larger cultural struggles.

If the new historicists had their way and managed to change the praxis of literary criticism so that all criticism were written with a concern for larger social, cultural, and political issues and with the intention of inducing change in the world at large, the result would not only be that such criticism would fail to have the intended effect (for all of the reasons just rehearsed), but the academic world would suffer a great loss: we would lose the skill and practice of close reading that make our work both unique and uniquely valuable. It is close reading with particular attention to the linguistic and semantic density of a work that gives the act of literary criticism its distinctive character and that constitutes its contribution to intellectual life. Fish laments that were that transformation to happen, something very precious will have died.[4]

Cultural Studies and the Appeal to Interdisciplinarity

> If cultural studies tells us to look elsewhere to find the meaning of the literary text, I say that if you look elsewhere, you will see something else.
> —Stanley Fish

> Cultural studies, it would seem, has replaced poetry as the replacement for religion; it is the new altar before which those who would cast off their infirmities worship.
> —Stanley Fish

The same arguments that Fish makes in the Clarendon Lectures against the hopes and objectives of the new historicists apply to the hopes and objectives of those who advocate cultural studies. While both groups aspire to transform literary studies into a more socially and politically relevant and effective discipline, cultural studies brings with it additional desires, assumptions, and objectives. Cultural studies is relentlessly interdisciplinary—some would say "counter-disciplinary." It regards the compartmentalizing of the production, dissemination, and consumption of knowledge into discrete disciplines as one way in which the dominant forces of society maintain hegemony over the oppressed. That is, to the extent that knowledge is kept fragmented and specialized, it becomes increasingly more difficult to comprehend the whole picture of oppression that constitutes the lives of most citizens on a daily basis. The university is complicitous in this effort in that it maintains and polices rigid disciplinary borders and regulates the production, dissemination, and consumption of knowledge. Cultural studies seeks to overcome the fragmentation of knowledge by claiming to take the entire social "text" as its object of study. Every cultural artifact, representation, and text, then, is a potential object of examination in cultural studies analysis. Of course, one implication of this perspective is that the effort by English studies to cordon off literary analysis as its own and to separate the texts of literature (high art) from those of popular culture (low art) is part of the struggle to maintain hegemony through the continued fragmentation of knowledge.

In effect, then, cultural studies—whether explicitly or implicitly—endeavors to create a kind of master discipline, a grand synthesis of all other disciplines. Fish finds at least two critical flaws in such claims. In declaring that all other disciplines are fragmentary and overly specialized but that cultural studies will somehow lead to a clearer perspective on the world, cultural studies is in effect asserting its superiority over all other disciplines: others are fragmented, partial, and disjointed; it is unified, whole, and complete. Other disciplines will lead only to partial vision, incomplete knowledge; cultural studies will lead to a larger perspective, more comprehensive knowledge. Elevating one discipline above all others is not only an instance of inexcusable academic hubris, it is clearly misguided. There is no legitimate hierarchy of academic jobs or disciplines. Academic work is divided into discrete disciplines precisely because each area performs a specific task or set of tasks, intellectual work that is unique and particular to itself. It is the particularity of such work that justifies a discipline's existence in the first place. The different jobs in academic work serve specific functions and are not capable, in Fish's view, of being ranked; they are simply different.

For similar reasons, the attempt to unify all knowledge in one master field is destined to fail. While the drive toward "interdisciplinarity" may sound like a noble endeavor (Fish suggests that at times it is professed with religious fervor), the very distinctiveness of tasks from discipline to discipline will militate against unification. Put simply, disciplinary self-preservation will exert pressure against the discipline's being subsumed in some larger endeavor. A discipline will strive to protect the unique kind of work it does from being appropriated or from being lost forever. Fish firmly believes that an intellectual discipline does not and will not simply choose to be partners in some utopian project that is likely to endanger its well-being. He insists that "whenever there is an apparent *rapproachement* or relationship of co-operation between projects, it will be the case either that one is anxiously trading on the prestige and vocabulary of the other or that one has swallowed the other; and this will be true not only when one project is academic and the other political, but when both are housed in the academy, perhaps in the same building" (83). A discipline is constituted by its specific traditions, histories, techniques, vocabularies, and methods of inquiry; in fact, we cannot even conceive a discipline apart from these defining characteristics. Once one discipline borrows from another—be it a theory, a vocabulary, or a mode of inquiry—the appropriating discipline immediately transforms the borrowed material into its own.

Some critics contend that because literature derives from a specific cultural context and simultaneously is defined by and helps to define that context, the best way to understand a literary text is to shift focus to the larger cultural context. Fish responds to this argument by claiming that shifting focus to the "background array of social practices" behind literature will not solve anything; it will only replace the original object of study with a new one that itself will then require explanation of what is "behind" *it*—a process that will extend on and on in an infinite regress. Because there will always be some "hidden" cause behind what is "seen," shifting focus from a literary text to a cultural text does not get us any closer to the deeper underlying causes of a text; it only shifts attention from one object to another. What's more, the shift in focus to a "cultural text" is not, in Fish's view, a shift to an epistemologically or ontologically superior text; it is simply a shift to a *different* text. And this different text brings with it "its own emphases, details, and meanings which 'naturally' crowd out the emphases, details, and meanings of other texts." That is, focusing on the cultural text will not "provide a deeper apprehension of the literary text or the legal text; rather it will erase them even in the act of referring to them, for the references will always be produced from *its* angle of interest, not theirs" (79). Put simply, a move toward cultural studies would be disciplinary suicide for literary studies.

Because a discipline acquires its identity from being uniquely qualified to perform one set of tasks that others are not in the position to perform (not all tasks or any tasks but a set of tasks specific to its own competence), a discipline necessarily, then, does *not* perform a great many other tasks—tasks that do not lie within the scope of its own work. If a discipline pays undue attention to the relationship between and among disciplines, it will likely diminish its capacity to perform its own distinctive set of tasks. And if a discipline diminishes its capacity to perform its own distinctive set of tasks, it will begin to lose its immanent intelligibility and thus its usefulness to anyone external to itself: the academy or the larger society. This is precisely the threat that Fish believes interdisciplinary studies poses, especially to English studies.

Those who advocate cultural studies and its interdisciplinary approach argue that disciplinary integrity is an illusion and therefore not worth defending in the way that Fish does throughout the lectures. They contend that all disciplines are social constructions and so the "unity" or immanent intelligibility of disciplines is illusory. In reply, Fish claims that academic disciplines are indeed social constructions but that this fact does not make them any less real. While disciplines—the carving up of intellectual tasks into discrete sets—are human creations rather than reflections of "nature," they nonetheless have force. Saying that disciplinary boundaries are social constructions only explains how the boundaries got there, not that they shouldn't exist or that they shouldn't exist in their present form. And the same is true about the unity of disciplines. Pointing out that a discipline's immanent intelligibility is arbitrary or that it changes over time does not make that unity disappear; it only explains how that unity is constituted: "Just because the unity is underwritten by rhetoric rather than by nature or logic in no way lessens the force of its operation in the moments of its existence. So long as it is even temporarily established, the unity of a discipline has a material existence and therefore has material effects that no analysis can dispel" (74). In fact, the very fact that disciplines are *social* constructions indicates that their form and content are not simply self-generated; rather, they "become perspicuous by virtue of relationships (of similarity and difference) with other disciplines that are themselves relationally, not essentially, constituted" (75). One implication of this fact is that a group within a discipline—cultural studies specialists, for example—cannot simply will a discipline to become something that it is not. As Fish comments in the interview in chapter 5, one can't simply wake up one morning and say, "Today, I will redefine the context of work within which I've been engaged."

Redefining the context of the intellectual work of English studies, however, is precisely the agenda of many cultural studies specialists. They hope to transform literary studies so that it is more deeply and directly connected with contemporary political issues and struggles, including sexism, racism, and homophobia. Such work, they hope, will lead to substantive political and social change. Fish's reply to these critics is exactly the same as his argument against the objectives of the new historicists outlined above: when critics are operating *as* academics within the constraints and forums of the discipline, they will necessarily be reaching only a relatively small number of people (their colleagues in the discipline) and thus will have little or no political effectiveness; conversely, if they depart from the usual modes of expression, methodologies, and forums of the discipline and thereby discover some degree of political effectivity outside of the academy, they will no longer be operating as critics: they will be operating as something *other* than critics. Of course, the objection could then be made that it is not up to Fish or anyone else to decide "what we do around here." One might ask why "academic work" can't simply be enlarged to encompass not just the usual types of tasks but also tasks involving the struggle for social change. Fish's answer to this challenge is that what constitutes a discipline's "work" is certainly not up to any one person or group of people; it is decided by the discipline as a whole. If we were to successfully expand what counts as academic work, we would eventually reach a point where "academic work" means every kind of work—and thus no specific work at all: if the "category of 'academic work' were enlarged to the point that it included almost anything an academic did—whether in the classroom, the jury box, or the town hall—the category would have no content because it would contain everything" (87). Political work and academic work, though occasionally overlapping, are distinct from one another.

Fish notes that while it is true that three forms of academic study—feminism, African American studies, and gay and lesbian studies—seem to have particularly close links to transformations occurring in contemporary society, there is little evidence that *academic* work in these areas has led to specific social or political change. The civil rights movement and the struggles for women's rights and for gay rights did not originate in the academy; rather, they began as social movements in the world external to the academy, and the academic areas of study associated with them emerged in response to and support of these ongoing struggles. Thus, when changes in society are already occurring, "academic work can be linked up to them by agents who find the formulations of that work politically useful," but this scenario in no way equates with academic work—scholarly books, journal articles, conference presentations—effecting or even affecting social or cultural change. In effect, these academic areas of study "piggy-back" on the larger social movements already in progress.[5]

While the aspiration of most cultural studies proponents is to bring about social change, usually in the form of greater social justice, many would settle for a less ambitious accomplishment: to help increasingly more people develop "critical self-consciousness." The critically aware person understands that "truth" is contingent and socially constructed, and this understanding is itself thought to be emancipatory. It is not that the critically aware person can escape the force of ideology; it's that critical awareness makes a qualitative difference in one's life. This appeal to critical self-consciousness is a common theme in much cultural studies literature. For Fish, however, there simply is no such thing as critical self-consciousness.[6] Being critically aware in the way that it is typically described would necessarily entail simultaneously understanding that one is embedded in ideology and somehow mentally floating free of that embeddedness,[7] and this is inconceivable:

> Critical self-consciousness, conceived of as a mental action independent of the setting in which it occurs, is the last infirmity of the mind that would deny its own limits by positioning itself in two places at the same time, in the place of its local embodiment and in the disembodied place (really no place) of reflection. It is to this latter place that cultural studies promises to bring us by relaxing the grip of forms of thought and categorization specific to particular disciplines. (104)

The particular form of cognitive activity that we term reflection, then, is central to cultural studies; in fact, Fish sees cultural studies as the attempt to institutionalize this activity. It's not that he believes that reflection itself is impossible; he in fact acknowledges that it is a common activity for most of us. He believes, however, that some cultural studies proponents have made claims for reflection that it couldn't possibly make good on. He contends that reflection does not float above the practices that are its object and thus provide "a vantage-point from which those practices can be assessed and reformed." Instead, reflection is "either (*a*) an activity *within* a practice and therefore finally not distanced from that practice's normative assumptions or (*b*) an activity grounded in its own normative assumptions and therefore one whose operations will reveal more about itself than about any practice viewed through its lens" (106). That is, no amount of critical self-consciousness will enable people to achieve the kind of distance from their practices and assumptions that cultural studies advertises as being the result of its work.

Public Intellectuals and the Work of English Studies

> Almost everyone wants to speak to more people, but the
> trick is getting those people to listen or even to hear you.
> —Stanley Fish

> The public justification of academic practices is too
> important a task to be left to academics.
> —Stanley Fish

A central theme reiterated by new historicists and cultural studies
specialists alike is that a principal way for academics to make their voice
heard by society at large and thereby enable them to influence social
change is to resurrect the notion of the public intellectual: someone that
the public consistently turns to for insight on any number of subjects. A
public intellectual would expound not only on issues deriving from his or
her academic area but on a wide range of subjects relevant to a broad
audience, and such a person would do so by gaining access to forums of
dissemination outside the confines of the academy—national television,
newspapers, and magazines, for instance. Throughout the Clarendon
Lectures, Fish repeats his contention that such hopes are unrealizable. It
is not evident, for example, how one *becomes* a public intellectual in the
first place. If it were simply a matter of choice, many of those who are
calling for a return of the public intellectual would already enjoy greater
access to the public. In addition, becoming a public intellectual is not
exclusively a matter of gaining access to forums of communication; one
then somehow has to ensure that people will *listen*. The fact is that given
the structural relations between the academy and the larger public, no
reliable avenue exists for preparing oneself for such a role. As Fish points
out, there is "no degree to be had, no accepted course of accreditation, no
departments of Public Relevance" (117). One might choose to become a
public intellectual, but, after having made such a choice, there is no
established procedure or formula that would dependably lead to that
desired result.

A central defining characteristic of the public intellectual is that such
a person can command the public's attention, and, according to Fish, this
factor alone disqualifies most academics. By definition, academics are
marginalized within the confines of the academy, and the academy—the
so-called ivory tower—is not a likely or even suitable forum from which
to command a large public audience. Becoming an academic, then, is not

an appropriate strategy for becoming a public intellectual: "Since one cannot gain that attention from the stage of the academy (except by some happy contingency), academics, by definition, are not candidates for the role of public intellectual. Whatever the answer to the question, 'How does one get to be a public intellectual?' we know that it *won't* be 'by joining the academy'" (118).

Fish is quick to point out that it is certainly true that a sizable number of academics do appear in public and address a large audience. To illustrate, he cites a lengthy list of academics who would be familiar to most people who pay attention to the popular media—a list that includes Catherine MacKinnon, Edward Said, and Carl Sagan. But such individuals are not public intellectuals in the usual sense of the term; instead, they are what Fish calls "cameo" or "rent for a day" intellectuals. Cameo intellectuals are academics who are invited to appear on a given television talk show or to write a particular op-ed piece for a national newspaper because they are considered authorities on the issue in question. Typically, such forums pair off two or more academics with opposing viewpoints so as to increase the interest level of the program; that is, such forums appear to be more about entertainment and ratings than about delving deeply or substantively into complex intellectual subjects. Cameo intellectuals are only given a forum when a particular issue enters the news; otherwise, they have little or no access to large public forums.[8] This model hardly matches the usual sense of what it means to be a public intellectual. For Fish, a public intellectual is "the *public's* intellectual": someone to whom the public "regularly looks for illumination on any number of (indeed all) issues." As things stand now, however, the public "does not look to academics for this *general* wisdom, in part because (as is often complained) academics are not trained to speak on everything, only on particular things, but more importantly because academics do not have a stage or a pulpit from which their pronouncements, should they be inclined to make them, could be broadcast" (119). In short, the structural relations between the academy and the available public forums of communication are such that the call for the return of the public intellectual is naive at best.

From time to time an academic will become influential outside of the academy—at least temporarily. Alan Bloom comes to mind, and Fish cites the case of Leo Strauss, the conservative political philosopher who railed against the dangerous relativism of postmodern thought. A host of individuals in the Reagan and Bush administrations picked up on Strauss' views, and, as a consequence, his perspectives had great purchase for a number of years. And, of course, from time to time academics will leave the university to accept positions in government, thereby exerting some influence. The salient point, however, is that while it is always *possible* for an academic to exert influence through his or her work or through securing an appointment outside of the academy, there is no reliable and customary avenue by which this can be accomplished:

> But if these men and women were influential it was not because of their teachings and writings but because they managed through non-academic connections to secure positions that gave their teachings and writings a force that they would not have had if they had remained in the academy where they would have had to wait for some accidental meeting between their "great thoughts" and the powers that be. Absent such an accident or an appointment to public office only contingently related to those thoughts (government officials don't say, "He wrote a great book on the English novel; let's make him Secretary of Education"), there are no regular routes by which the accomplishments of academics in general and literary academics in particular can be transformed into the currency of politics. (97)

Commanding a large public audience and connecting one's work up to that audience is simply not a matter of will; it is a matter of chance. Given the seemingly insurmountable barriers to transforming the world by becoming a public intellectual, Fish advises that literary critics seek their satisfaction in the pleasures of producing literary criticism (and, to Fish, such pleasures are abundant); otherwise, he warns, they will face a lifetime of constant frustration as the desire to extend the influence of their work into "precincts incapable of recognizing" or responding to it will go "forever unrealized" (98).[9]

The aspirations of those who seek to influence public policy aside, there will always be a need to justify academic work to the public, to demonstrate that "what we do around here" is of value and therefore deserves support. That is, while abandoning the distinctive work that defines our contribution to society in search of some wider, less-well-articulated influence on the public would be fatal, severing all connections with the public would be just as detrimental. In fact, justifying academic work to the public is essential to a discipline's continued well-being. Especially at a time of shrinking budgets and demands for accountability, a discipline cannot merely content itself with *self*-justification. This need to speak to the public about our distinctive contributions, however, is at odds with our inability to speak to the public as public intellectuals. Fish writes,

> If academics are unsuited, both by inclination and training, for the role of public intellectual, and if access to that role is usually gained by routes not open to most academics (unless they happen to inherit a radio station), and if those who now occupy that role are either hostile or indifferent to academic practices, and if academic practices are regularly under attack and therefore in need of articulate and well-positioned defenders, what are we to do? (125–26)[10]

Although Fish's answer to this question surprised a number of people when he first uttered it, no one should have been surprised, since his answer is entirely consistent with his argument in the Clarendon Lectures: he recommends that departments follow the lead of the Modern Language Association and hire lobbyists to promote the merit and significance of their praxis. The distinctiveness of tasks that makes the members of a discipline uniquely qualified to do a particular kind of work is what makes those members "professionals." If departments of English sincerely wish to promote their worth to the public and to legislators and to boards of regents, they should not trust this important work to amateurs—that is, to academics; rather, they should entrust it to professionals, those who are uniquely qualified to undertake such work. A professional lobbyist who lets "no opportunity go begging" and allows "no accusation to go unanswered" would be the most successful and effective promoter of academic values to a non-academic public.[11]

Fish and His Discontents

> I would like to provide this book with two directions for the user. 1. Do not read it as evidence that I have changed my mind or my politics. 2. Do not read it as a repudiation of cultural studies, black studies, feminist studies, gay and lesbian studies, and other forms of activity that have reinvigorated the literary scene.
> —Stanley Fish

> My support for non-traditional scholarship in the humanities is as strong as it ever was.
> —Stanley Fish

Many of the arguments that found their fullest articulation in *Professional Correctness* were first presented at the Nineteenth Alabama Symposium on English and American Literature in 1993.[12] Fish's contribution, "Them We Burn: Violence and Conviction in the English Department," apparently stunned both audience and participants alike and later became the focal point of the conference's published proceedings, James Raymond's *English as a Discipline: Or, Is There a Plot in this Play?* The conference organizer reported that Fish's entry into "the fray" had the effect of "instantly polarizing the audience like so many iron filings pointing resolutely toward either love or hate" (Raymond 5). Many of the conference contributors used the occasion of the published proceedings to articulate critiques of Fish's position. Phyllis Frus, for example, understood Fish to be arguing that we should only produce New Critical "aesthetic readings," and she charged him with attempting to "police" the discipline's boundaries in an authoritarian manner: "I fear the conviction of one who is so sure he is right that he is willing to silence others who he 'knows' are wrong" (179). Paul Lauter found it "impossible to support Fish's absolute division of academic from political work," charging Fish with setting up a simplistic binary opposition that "obscures what we actually do both in figuring out what a poem 'means' and in carrying out political work" (184). Stanley Corkin accused Fish of being unaware of and standing apart from history, and he claimed that Fish had argued both sides of the debate on disciplinarity: that prior to the conference he had written in support of the new areas of research that were reinvigorating scholarship in the humanities, while at the conference he had argued (in Corkin's understanding) that critics should not do any other work than "what we are supposed to as English professors" (176).[13]

It was Gerald Graff, however, who most articulately and thoughtfully engaged Fish's arguments. He contended that English studies could never claim to be a "discipline" because its intellectual concerns "turn out to be too diverse to fit under a single disciplinary definition." But disciplinary status, in his view, should not even be a concern; what *should* be a major concern is whether English studies is "conceptually coherent." It would be a mistake, he argued, to confuse coherence with disciplinarity (11). That is, it is essential that English studies be able to justify itself to the public, and it can do so only by being able to present its diverse interests and projects as all somehow contributing to some larger mission. In his "Is There a Conversation in This Curriculum? Or, Coherence without Disciplinarity," Graff declares that it is embarrassing that most people outside of the academy do not understand "why there need to be professionalized departments armed with elaborately analytical methods in order to deal with books that—to all appearances—were written simply to be enjoyed" (11). So, while he agrees with Fish that English studies needs to justify its work to the public, unlike Fish he is confident that the field can easily contain the diverse interests that it has accumulated over time. In fact, he feels that English departments have "hardly begun to tap" the great "potential coherence in English studies" (12).

Despite Fish's belief that if English studies continues to widen its scope it will diminish its distinctiveness of tasks and thereby lose its ability to justify its existence, Graff argues that recent interdisciplinary and political scholarship has revitalized not only English studies but the humanities in general. What's more, English studies has for the first time found itself able to influence other disciplines, in that the "best of the boundary-crossing work in English and other literature departments (including prominent work by Fish himself and cogently defended by him against conservative attacks) has earned it a legitimate influence in disciplines such as law, philosophy, history, and anthropology" (13). Besides, argues Graff, it is simply untrue that political criticism has replaced formalistic or belletristic criticism; they coexist side by side. For Graff, the "return to literature" seems

> about as likely as a return to manual typewriters. It would require an abrupt renunciation of what is arguably the most enabling discovery of the next generation: that "literature" is not a closed category—to be counterposed against "ordinary language," as the New Critics used to do—but one that overlaps with and is permeated throughout by the concerns of philosophy, rhetoric, politics, sociology, law, psychology, and other disciplines. (14)

So, even if we desired to return to a more restrictive understanding of our distinct tasks, such a return is impossible; the field has already transformed itself in the directions that Fish fears it will.

Notwithstanding these and other critiques of Fish's arguments about disciplinary distinctiveness, it is difficult to disagree with his position *if you take those arguments on the terms that he sets out*. For example, despite the contention by Graff and others that interdisciplinary work and political criticism have helped reinvigorate the humanities, which seems to be quite clearly correct, Fish is equally correct in claiming that *literary* studies is distinct from all other intellectual work precisely because it undertakes the unique labor of analyzing *literary* works; that is, by definition it is *not* a study of popular culture or of society or of sociology or of any other subject. Similarly, Fish is indisputably correct in asserting that *literary* work is not *political* work, that when literary critics are operating *as* academics within the constraints and forums of the discipline, they will necessarily be reaching only a relatively small number of people (their colleagues in the discipline) and thus will have little or no political effectiveness; conversely, if they depart from the usual modes of expression, methodologies, and forums of the discipline and thereby discover some degree of political effectivity outside of the academy, they will no longer be operating as literary critics: they will be operating as something *other* than literary critics. And it seems equally futile to argue against Fish's contention that because literary critics are insulated within the confines of their specific subject areas as well as within the academy itself, they have no ready and regular access to national forums of communication or centers of political power. While many could and have challenged these arguments, such attempts are pointless because Fish has left very little to contest within the narrow contexts in which he has made his arguments: literary studies is by definition the study of *literary* works; when academics are writing about literary works to an audience of fellow academics, such work is unlikely to have political ramifications in the world at large; and, given the structural dynamics between the academy and society, literary critics simply have no conventional avenues of communication with the public or with politicians in positions of power. That is, the structural makeup of Fish's arguments are such that so long as we grant his context (literary studies), his contentions are unassailable.

What neither Fish nor his critics account for, however, is that English studies in the contemporary academy comprises more than just *literary* studies; it also includes the field of rhetoric and composition. The key to Fish's argument is the term *literary*. So long as the focus is exclusively on literary studies—on the analysis of literary texts—then by definition Fish's claims and the conclusions arising from them are irrefutable. But because English studies encompasses not only the consumption and analysis of text but also the production of discourse, some—but not all— of Fish's arguments might need to be qualified. Certainly, the fact that English studies also comprises rhetoric and composition has no bearing on his critique of new historicism. Nor does it affect his argument that when (in this case) English professors are operating *as* academics within the constraints and forums of the discipline, they will necessarily be reaching only a relatively small number of people and thus will have little or no political effectiveness. Nor does it invalidate his claim that those of us engaged in intellectual work in English studies have no ready and regular access to national forums of communication or centers of power. And, of course, it has no bearing on the fact that the once-strong link between academic work and the "public intellectual" no longer exists.

The fact that English studies also includes the field of rhetoric and composition *does* affect, however, Fish's arguments about the role of cultural studies—but only in a weak way. Fish is right to assert that elevating one discipline above all others is an instance of academic hubris, that there is no legitimate hierarchy of academic jobs or disciplines; and given the entrenched structure of the academy, any attempt to unify all knowledge in one master field is destined to fail. What's more, the claim that cultural studies can somehow lead to grand changes in society are naive for all the reasons Fish delineates. Yet, all of this does *not* mean that cultural studies can play no legitimate role in English studies. Fish objects to the introduction of cultural studies because it threatens the immanent intelligibility, the distinctiveness, of English studies. And this would be entirely true if the discipline really only encompassed literary studies. However, any threat to the immanent intelligibility of English studies must be evaluated according to whether the new direction—in this case cultural studies—somehow does or does not conform to "what we do around here"; and since part of "what we do around here" includes the intellectual work of rhetoric and composition, it is necessary to consider whether cultural studies would detract from the distinctiveness of that part of English studies before concluding that it has no role to play whatsoever.

Now, it is certainly true that some people might argue that rhetoric and composition itself suffers from its own problems with immanent intelligibility because it is such a large and sprawling field of inquiry, ranging from investigations into the cognitive processes of writers to speculation about the workings of ideology and discourse to examinations of how technology alters both writing and our relationship to it. Yet, most scholars within the field would agree with this broad definition: that rhetoric and composition is devoted both to interrogating how written discourse works and to exploring how best to help students learn to achieve greater facility in composing their own discourse. That is, rhetoric and composition is that part of English studies that is most concerned with the production of discourse, while literary studies is the part most concerned with the consumption and analysis of discourse, primarily *literary* discourse. Put more simply, together we are jointly concerned with writing and reading.

Unlike literary studies, rhetoric and composition does not begin with a specific methodology that it then applies to a clearly defined object of inquiry. Rather, it takes as its object of study all of written discourse. Thus, not only is it entirely within the scope of its work to examine the rhetoric of certain cultural texts, it is also entirely appropriate—and a standard practice of many—to employ cultural texts within the composition classroom both as objects of rhetorical analysis and as fodder for students' own writing.[14] A cultural studies orientation, then, is already part of "what we do around here" in both the scholarship and the pedagogy of rhetoric and composition. So, while large-scale importation of cultural studies into literary studies would, as Fish suggests, erode or even destroy the distinctiveness of literary studies, attenuating the specific set of tasks that literary critics perform and that set them apart from other academics, this would not be (and has not been) true of the typically neglected part of English studies: rhetoric and composition.

I am not the first to point out that Fish's conception of English studies is restricted to literary studies. Sidney Dobrin writes in a review essay in *College English*: "I find it remarkable that neither in this contribution ["Them We Burn"] nor in *Professional Correctness* does Fish turn to composition studies, to the teaching of writing, in his understanding of what we do in English departments. Fish is remiss in not identifying the importance of composition studies—and more importantly composition's inherently interdisciplinary nature—when he discusses the singular task which earns our position at the table of tasks" (696). Nevertheless, on a certain level it is understandable that someone with an academic pedigree like that of Fish would "forget" or not even recognize that rhetoric and composition is now an integral part of English studies.[15] Fish earned his three degrees from Ivy League institutions (the University of Pennsylvania and Yale), and he has taught at such prestigious institutions as Berkeley, Johns Hopkins, and Duke. While rhetoric and composition has a strong disciplinary presence in English departments throughout the country, it is still resisted and marginalized in the nation's most distinguished universities, including all of those just mentioned. Given the fact that rhetoric and composition is not a strong part of the departments with which he is most familiar, it is no surprise that he does not address its presence when he discusses the workings of English departments.

Nor is Fish alone; most literary scholars of his stature who have recently contemplated the nature and future of English studies have similarly ignored this subdiscipline. There *are* a few exceptions, however. For many years, J. Hillis Miller has called for more integration of English studies' two main components, and Gerald Graff not only acknowledges the importance of rhetoric and composition, he also calls for those concerned about the future of English studies to structure a dialogue between literary studies and composition studies (26). Perhaps Graff is correct: more dialogue between literary studies and rhetoric and composition will go a long way in helping the discipline to construct a more realistic and balanced understanding of "what we do around here." Nevertheless, the fact remains that most major discussions of the future of English studies simply ignore the role of rhetoric and composition. What this neglect bodes for the future of English studies remains to be seen, but inevitably rhetoric and composition will need to be factored into any analysis of the future of the discipline. Perhaps the growing alliance between rhetoric and composition and cultural studies will indicate how the latter can find a home in the contemporary English department without eroding the discipline's immanent intelligibility—an intelligibility that includes the intellectual work of rhetoric and composition.

Even though Fish does not factor rhetoric and composition into his analysis, he does present a powerful and cogent argument about how we in English studies, if we are not careful, may lose our distinctiveness and thus our value both to the academy and to society in general. He demonstrates convincingly that if we forget or underestimate or fail to comprehend the importance of the field's immanent intelligibility to its continued existence and thus allow its borders to expand immeasurably, then the discipline may very well lose its distinct shape; and if English studies does lose its distinctiveness and thus is no longer able to claim that it performs tasks useful to anyone beyond its own borders, its days are numbered. Regardless of our particular take on new historicism, cultural studies, or public intellectuals, Fish provides an admonition that must be considered seriously, since it concerns our very existence. We dismiss his warning at our own peril.

Chapter 2

No Loss, No Gain:
The Argument against Principle

Fish has written an impressive number of works on a wide variety of subjects, from jurisprudence and hate speech to the nature of literary interpretation and the discipline of English, but a considerable number of his works cluster around a single argument: that general principles do not and cannot inform specific practice. He has applied this argument in numerous instances for an assortment of disparate audiences, addressing literary theorists about the role of theory, compositionists about the efficacy of composition theory, legal scholars about the function of principle, and multiculturalists about the limits of tolerance. As he says in the interview in chapter 5, "There are a lot of people out there making mistakes, and I'm just going to tell them that they're making mistakes. The mistakes are so deeply ingrained in the very forms of their own thought, however, that I'm in no danger of being persuasive, and I'm therefore in no danger of running out of occasions on which to make this limited—as I call it in a new essay, 'parsimonious'—argument." Perhaps the best way to understand these mistakes and the cluster of related arguments Fish makes to rectify them is to examine his argument about the role of theory.

35

The Illusory Consequences of Theory

> I have nothing to sell, except the not-very-helpful news,
> if it is news, that practice has nothing to do with theory,
> at least in the sense of being enabled and justified by
> theory.
>
> —Stanley Fish

> That is, no one follows or consults his formal model of the
> skill he is exercising in order properly to exercise it.
>
> —Stanley Fish

While Fish has made his so-called "anti-theory" point in a substantial number of works, the essay "Consequences" stands out as a tour de force of his reasoning on the subject. In characterizing this essay, Geoffrey Harpham has written, "What bravura spirit, what dazzling intelligence, what boldness, what eagerness for argumentation! Reading 'Consequences,' any reader must be impressed with the energy and inventiveness with which Fish prosecutes his case" (86). Despite the dazzling display of argumentative prowess, however, Fish's thesis is rather straightforward: he contends that while the objective of most theories is to elucidate, inform, or improve practice, a theory will not substantively affect the practice it considers.

The appeal to theory, both in literary criticism as well as in other disciplines, is a project that attempts to establish universal rules that regulate a particular practice. The conventional understanding of theory is that it is an effort to set aside all personal bias and self interest in order to discern and then codify the rules or principles by which something works. The theorist, then, is thought to be in a position of objectivity *outside* the workings of the practice in question and is thus able to distinguish, comprehend, and then formalize the rules or principles that govern the practice. Others can then appeal to these rules as a prescription for performing that practice in the future or for improving the practice. According to this traditional view, then, a theory is an effort to "*guide* practice from a position above or outside it" and to "*reform* practice by neutralizing interest, by substituting for the parochial perspective of some local or partisan point of view the perspective of a general rationality to which the individual subordinates his contextually conditioned opinions and beliefs" (319).

For Fish, the paradigmatic example of traditional—or what we have come to call "foundational"—theorizing is Chomskian linguistics, the project by which linguists attempt to discover the set of innate rules or constraints that enable speakers to produce an infinite number of grammatical utterances. These rules are thought to originate not in culture but in human nature and thus are not affected by race, gender, social class, geographical location, and so on; they derive, instead, from the so-called hard wiring in the human brain. As such, these rules transcend the variables and vagaries of quotidian human existence; they are universal and unchanging. Consequently, they can be studied and formalized, and once formalized they can serve as a method to improve the practice of utterance (as in the attempt to employ transformational grammar as a pedagogical method in composition classes). Chomskian linguistics is the perfect example of traditional, foundationalist theorizing, then, because it endeavors to produce a finite set of rules for a practice that when followed will always produce the exact same results.

The argument against theory is by now commonplace in intellectual circles, having been made by countless scholars in undoubtedly every academic discipline: the attempt to devise a theory—a set of universal rules governing a practice—is a futile enterprise, an example of the Enlightenment project par excellence. There is simply no way to separate the observer from the observed, no way to obtain knowledge unmediated by context and local contingencies. The theorist is always already deeply embedded in a context, and no theorist can merely, through an act of will, extract him or herself from that context so that he or she is positioned to observe and understand a practice apart from that context. As Fish says,

> Theory is an impossible project which will never succeed. It will never succeed simply because the primary data and formal laws necessary to its success will always be spied or picked out from within the contextual circumstances of which they are supposedly independent. The objective facts and rules of calculation that are to ground interpretation and render it principled are themselves interpretive products: they are, therefore, always and already contaminated by the interested judgments they claim to transcend. (320)

While the traditional theorist claims to transcend context and to dwell in the universal, no human being is capable of such transcendence; there is simply no way to escape or rise above the practice that one is engaged in. The content of a theory is always derived from the ever-changing world of practice, beliefs, assumptions, private values, and personal perspectives—from the local. Consequently, a theory will always fail to make good on its claim to provide a set of rules independent of the practice it describes; and because a theory will always fail in its goal to guide and reform practice, it therefore, by definition, can have no consequence.

In the case of Chomskian linguistics, for example, the effort to compile a set of rules that govern how all sentences work (rules that are independent of context) is destined to fail because it is literally impossible to find sentences that do not derive from a speaker's history, beliefs, assumptions, private values, and personal perspectives—from the local, contingent circumstances of the speaker. As Fish points out, such sentences just do not exist. While a linguist may very well present a sentence that seems intelligible independent of an individual speaker's context, it does not follow that somehow that sentence has escaped the context within which it was produced; rather, such a case only illustrates that the context is so firmly entrenched, so sedimented, that the context has become invisible. Fish writes, "Linguistic knowledge is contextual rather than abstract, local rather than general, dynamic rather than invariant; every rule is a rule of thumb; every competence grammar is a performance grammar in disguise" (321).[1]

If Fish had ended his argument against theory with this rather common assault on foundationalist theory, he would be one among a multitude of scholars who have made similar cases over the last quarter of a century, but he in fact extends this identical reasoning to anti-foundationalist theory as well. That is, the effort to demonstrate that it is impossible to set aside all personal bias and self-interest in order to discern and then codify the rules or principles by which something works is itself subject to the same critique. While foundationalist theory can have no consequences in the real world of practice, neither can anti-foundationalist theory have any consequences.

Traditional theorists are animated by what Fish calls "theory hope," the desire and expectation that their claims to knowledge can be justified by an objective method of evaluating those claims, a method that rises above the individual circumstances of the people making the claims. Anti-foundationalists, in Fish's view, suffer from their own version of theory hope: the desire to free us from the confining fetters of groundless universals, unfounded absolutes, and contextless rules by demonstrating "the contextual source of conviction." Such a desire will be thwarted, however, because the "fact that we now have a new explanation of how we got our beliefs—the fact, in short, that we now have a new belief—does not free us from our other beliefs or cause us to doubt them" (324). The fact that you discover that a belief that you strongly hold arises from your education, training, and socioeconomic class status, say, is not likely to dislodge that belief; it simply makes you conscious of how you came about the belief in the first place. Even if someone were to demonstrate to you that a certain belief that you adhere to had its origin in a perspective personally repugnant to you and you then altered or rejected that belief, this would not constitute an instance of theory being the source of conviction in the large or strong sense; rather, it would constitute a very specific alteration of belief in a very circumscribed instance. Such an instance would be, according to Fish, "a quite specific reconsideration provoked by a perceived inconsistency in my beliefs (and it would have to be an inconsistency that struck me as intolerable), not a general reconsideration of my beliefs in the face of a belief about their source" (324). What's more, believing that people can and will alter their convictions based on some general proposition about how beliefs arise (a theory) is inconsistent with anti-foundationalist thinking itself, in that the very core tenet of such thought is that one does not operate from general principles independent of one's context. Thus, the goal of anti-foundationalist reasoning is unrealizable, and, so, like foundationalist theory, it too can have no consequences in the world of practice.

The flip side of theory hope is theory fear, a phenomenon usually associated with or leveled against anti-foundationalism. The effort to demonstrate that it is impossible to generate a general theory regulating how a practice operates independent of local contingencies—that is, anti-foundationalist thought—has provoked a great deal of trepidation, especially among conservative thinkers. People worry that those who subscribe to such a belief will likely become nihilists or radical relativists, relinquishing all constraints on professional and even personal behavior; in intellectual matters, all rational, principled inquiry would be abandoned for personal, idiosyncratic criteria of judgment. But such results do not and cannot follow from anti-foundationalist thought, according to Fish. Anti-foundationalist thought is not an argument for unchecked subjectivity or for the absence of constraints on individuals; it is exactly the opposite: it is an argument "for the situated subject, for the individual who is always constrained by the local or community standards and criteria of which his judgment is an extension" (323). That is, one lesson of anti-foundationalism is that local practice is always already guided by constraints; it's just that these constraints are local "rules of thumb" rather than universal principles. Fish writes,

> Thus the lesson of anti-foundationalism is not only that external and independent guides will never be found but that it is unnecessary to seek them, because you will always be guided by the rules or rules of thumb that are the content of any settled practice, by the assumed definitions, distinctions, criteria of evidence, measures of adequacy, and such, which not only define the practice but structure the understanding of the agent who thinks of himself as a "competent member." That agent cannot distance himself from these rules, because it is only within them that he can think about alternative courses of action or, indeed, think at all. (323)

Because the lesson of anti-foundationalism is that action is in fact constrained (it's just not constrained in the way that foundationalists had assumed), it cannot possibly have the consequences that those who succumb to theory fear had prophesied. Consequently, both the hope of those who espouse anti-foundationalism (that it can free us from the confining fetters of groundless universals, unfounded absolutes, and contextless rules by demonstrating the contextual source of conviction) and the fear of those who loathe anti-foundationalism (that it can free us from the confining fetters of groundless universals, unfounded absolutes, and contextless rules by demonstrating the contextual source of conviction) are unrealizable. In a word, anti-foundationalism simply cannot have any consequences in the world of practice.

Fish, as usual, endeavors to articulate and then defuse the potential objections that readers might have to any given position he is arguing. Someone might declare, for instance, that it is unnecessary to restrict theory to foundationalist attempts to codify a set of operating rules for a practice and anti-foundationalist attempts to illustrate that such efforts are futile. For example, many literary critical works make claims that rise above or extend beyond the specific interpretations of particular works of literature. While neither foundationalist nor anti-foundationalist, such works might be considered theoretical in that they typically identify patterns or regularities that apply to multiple works of literature.[2] Such patterns, however, are not invariant or predictive; they do not hold for all literature at all times and provide a general and abstract picture of all such literature. Instead, they present information that is drawn from a finite corpus of works and that is relevant only to that corpus and in a circumscribed period of time. Rather than standing apart from local practice, such attempts derive directly from it and constitute "a report on its current shape or on the shape it once had in an earlier period" (325). Far from constituting theory in any strong sense, such literary critical works are perfect examples of practice in action.

In response, someone might ask why the kinds of generalizations made in such works could not simply be called theory even though they do not rise to the level of universality normally associated with traditional theory. But to call such generalizations theory, Fish argues, would be to expand the concept of theory so immeasurably that the concept would no longer have any specific meaning and would thus lose its usefulness. Generalizations that are theoretical in the conventional sense and those that are not would all be grouped under a single heading, and thus the notion of theory as a unique and special entity would cease to exist. And even if these kinds of weak generalizations had some general use value, as when a critical work influences other critics to entertain novel interpretations of certain literary works, such influence still does not rise to the level of universality that would warrant the appellation "theory"; such a process is still *practice* in the routine work-a-day way that we usually construe it. Writes Fish, "If we like, we can always call such imitations of a powerful practice 'theory,' but nothing whatsoever will have been gained, and we will have lost any sense that theory is special. After all, it is only if theory is special that the question of its consequences is in any way urgent" (326). In short, if everything is theory, then nothing is.

Nevertheless, some scholars argue precisely that—that everything *is* theory, that all practice derives from theoretical assumptions, that there is no such thing as acting independent of the structure of assumptions, beliefs, and values that makes a particular practice intelligible. Fish agrees that certainly any practice that one engages in will be conceivable only in relation to the structure of assumptions, beliefs, and values that make that practice intelligible; however, it does not follow from this fact that every practice is underwritten by a theory. Beliefs are not theories, and conflating them only confuses the issue. As Fish explains it,

> A theory is a special achievement of consciousness; a belief is a prerequisite for being conscious at all. Beliefs are not what you think *about* but what you think *with*, and it is within the space provided by their articulations that mental activity—including the activity of theorizing—goes on. Theories are something you can have—you can wield them and hold them at a distance; beliefs

have *you*, in the sense that there can be no distance between them
and the acts they enable. (326)

In short, we cannot act at all without beliefs; they are basic to our
functioning in the world, and it is exactly our structure of beliefs that
enables us to engage in a practice in the first place, that underwrites that
practice. Theories, in contrast, rise to a much higher level of abstraction
and do not carry the weight or power of convictions.

Of course, not all beliefs are created equal. Some concern trivial
matters, while others may concern large ethical or philosophical questions. That is, some beliefs are the products of substantial contemplation
and even agonizing, while others are not. Regardless of the magnitude of
the issue or the amount of consideration given to it, however, a person's
belief is still a belief and not a theory. And while beliefs—large or
small—can cause someone to take certain actions or to behave in certain
ways, such behavior does not constitute acting according to a theory; it
constitutes acting according to one's beliefs. What's more, from time to
time a person may change his or her convictions about a particular subject
and, as a result, change the practice related to those beliefs, but even if
such a change in conviction and corresponding practice had some relation
to what might properly be called a theoretical position or a theory, we
cannot conclude that there is a strong causal relationship between the
theory and the change in conduct. As Fish points out, people can and do
change their minds and their practices for a multitude of reasons, but there
is no necessary connection or unique relationship between such a change
and a particular theory. A person can be moved to reexamine the
assumptions and beliefs undergirding his or her practice by any number
of factors, even factors unrelated to the practice ("by turning forty, or by
a dramatic alteration in one's economic situation, by a marriage, or by a
divorce"), but there is no unique relationship between such self-reflection
and a corresponding change in beliefs. In fact, one is just as likely after
being shown that a certain assumption is inconsistent or misguided to
shrug off such insight and to decide to live with the status quo. Thus, a
theory "cannot provide us with a perspective independent of our
beliefs, and the perspective it can occasionally (but not necessarily)
provide on some of our beliefs relative to others can be provided by
much that is not theory" (332, 333).

Despite the force and perspicuity of Fish's argument against theory,
a substantial number of scholars in every discipline still have faith that
theory, especially anti-foundationalist theory, will liberate us from the

shackles of ignorance. Fish attributes this faith to the success that philosophy has had in convincing almost everyone—not only academics, but the public at large—that philosophy alone can provide the answers to our most passionate questions. Philosophy's general relevance seems to go unquestioned, and a great many people have come to believe that most human actions—especially academic practices—have philosophical grounding. But philosophy, Fish reminds us, is the name of an academic discipline, not a "natural" human activity. Just as literary criticism is a distinctive intellectual practice uniquely qualified to undertake the interpretation of literary works, philosophy is a distinctive intellectual practice uniquely qualified to contemplate "philosophical" questions. As he argues in the Clarendon Lectures, a literary critic is a particular kind of specialist, and all specialists are defined by the specific traditions, histories, techniques, vocabularies, and methods of inquiry of their specializations. It seems counterintuitive to argue that a specialist in one field, philosophy or any other, could improve or change the practice of a specialist in another. A literary critic is embedded in a specific praxis and produces a reading of a literary work within and because of this unique and specialized context. In fact, it is the very fact of being located within this specific praxis that marks a literary critic as a particular kind of specialist who joins other critics in jointly operating within a common field and by ways that are immediately intelligible to one another. While a critic could certainly choose to step back from a practice and ask of it the kinds of questions that "belong properly (that is, by history and convention) to philosophy," the lessons that the critic would learn from such an exercise "would be philosophical, not literary, and the fact that it was possible to learn them would not prove that those who do criticism are really doing philosophy" (334). In short, philosophy and literary criticism are two distinct enterprises, and conflating them serves no useful purpose. Yet, this is exactly what critics do when they make appeals to "theory," another name for philosophy. Despite the aesthetic, epistemological, or methodological differences among various kinds of literary critics, they are all engaged in a common activity and would recognize each other as so engaged despite their differences in proceeding. Theory, however, "disdains particular acts of interpretation and aspires to provide an account of interpretation in general—and just as a philosophical analysis of an activity is not an instance of that activity but of philosophy, so an account of interpretation is not an interpretation but an account" (335). Even if a literary critic borrows the vocabulary and concepts of another field—philosophy or any other—this does not constitute becoming a practitioner of that field, nor does it mean that the vocabulary or concepts of the field have consequentially changed the field's practice; rather, it has simply become "the passive object of appropriation." The fact that critics may very well now use a vocabulary of "aporias and radical de-centerings where they used to discover irony and unity," simply indicates, says Fish, that "thematizing remains the primary mode of literary criticism and that, as an action, thematizing can find its materials in theory as well as in anything else" (335–36). Fish concludes from this line of reasoning that even when a critic is also a theorist, theory simply has no consequence.

Having made the argument that as an effort to elucidate, inform, or improve practice from a position outside of that practice theory will not substantively affect the practice it considers, Fish does admit that there are certain limited ways in which theory can indeed have consequences, but these are not the consequences that those under the sway of either theory hope or theory fear desire or predict. Theory has consequences not in that it can guide or reform practice but precisely in that theory itself is a form of practice. That is, theorizing, along with its corresponding vocabulary and concepts, has become an integral part of the practice of literary criticism, the "kind of work we do around here." As such, it has had an effect on how the work of literary criticism gets done. It has not furnished a set of general principles governing the act of interpretation, it has not provided a prescription for reforming critical practice, and it has not liberated us from the confining fetters of groundless universals, unfounded absolutes, and contextless rules; it has, however, become part of the daily praxis of critics, and in that relatively modest way it has had some consequence. Just as Fish argues in the Clarendon Lectures that it is necessary to distinguish the general sense of the political (the sense in which on a certain level everything is contestable and therefore political) from the more substantive and consequential understanding of the political (the realm in which elections are won and lost, policies adopted or rejected, programs instituted or eliminated), so too is it necessary to distinguish the general sense of the consequential (the sense in which on a certain level every action can produce some effect) from the more substantive understanding of the consequential (the kind of effect in which disciplines are substantially transformed and heartfelt convictions are abandoned). Theory has and can only have consequence on this weak level.[3]

Lest someone accuse Fish of inconsistency, he scrupulously announces that he does not expect arguments such as his own attack on theory to have any practical effect in the world. Like any other theorizing, his case against both foundationalist and anti-foundationalist theory will necessarily have limited effect, if any. It does not provide an objective perspective on practice, it is not likely to change people's fervent convictions, and it will not reform critical practice. That is, the discrediting of theory will not return us to "some precritical state, whether it be thought of as a state of innocence or of know-nothing ignorance" (340). As he comments in the interview in chapter 5, "If after having read me or heard me you go away with something useful, I will have failed"—that is, he will have fallen into the same epistemological trap that he accuses others of falling into. In short, his "no consequences" argument simply will have no consequences.

Theory and the Teaching of Composition

> Not only does being converted to anti-foundationalism bring with it no pedagogical payoff; being opposed to anti-foundationalism entails no pedagogical penalty.
> —Stanley Fish

> Composition teachers are always teaching situations because they can do nothing else.
> —Stanley Fish

Fish's argument against theory's consequences extends to any number of areas within and outside of English studies. For example, concerned that theory hope (and theory fear) was capturing the imagination of scholars in rhetoric and composition, he set out to apply the same arguments to the teaching and practice of writing. In "Anti-Foundationalism, Theory Hope, and the Teaching of Composition," he points out that foundationalist theory sets out to ground both inquiry and communication itself in "something more firm and stable than mere belief or unexamined practice"; the strategy is to identify that ground and then to organize the activities involved in the teaching and practice of writing in such a way that they are anchored to that ground and thus objective and principled (342). That is, the successful foundationalist project in composition would construct a "model" of both writing and the teaching of writing; when the steps laid out by the model are followed scrupulously, the correct result will always be produced. The ground to which such a model can be moored can take any number of forms given the ideological and epistemological orientations of the compositionists seeking that ground, including "God, the material or 'brute act' world, rationality in general and logic in particular, a neutral-observation language, the set of eternal values, and the free and independent self" (343). Every foundationalist project, including those in composition, bases its research and pedagogical projects on one or more of these typical kinds of ground, according to Fish.

Although from its inception rhetoric and composition has been populated by many who sought to ground their projects either in neutral-observation language (the so-called cognitivists) or in the free and independent self (the so-called expressivists), it has also had its share of anti-foundationalists: those who believe that "questions of fact, truth, correctness, validity, and clarity can neither be posed nor answered in reference to some extracontextual, ahistorical, nonsituational reality, or rule, or law, or value." Instead, anti-foundationalist compositionists (like any anti-foundationalists) assert that all such matters are "intelligible and debatable only within the precincts of the contexts or situations or paradigms or communities that give them their local and changeable shape" (344). Anti-foundationalism in rhetoric and composition is most closely associated with those often called social constructionists—and, lately, with those advocating a "post-process paradigm"—and the anti-foundationalists made substantial progress during the late 1980s and the 1990s in moving the discipline closer to an anti-foundationalist orientation. Nevertheless, argues Fish, anti-foundationalist thought in composition has as little chance to accomplish its objectives as foundational thought does *its* goals.

It is not at all surprising that compositionists would seek a "methodological payoff" in anti-foundationalist thought. After all, such thought seems totally in keeping with the field's allegiance to process, with its movement away from a preoccupation with rules and strictures and toward teaching compositional strategies—that is, with its move toward rhetoric. At a certain level, there seems to be a "natural match" between anti-foundationalist thought and the process approach to composition—or, more accurately, the rhetorical approach to composition. In fact, for Fish "anti-foundationalism *is* rhetoric" (347). What's more, embracing anti-foundationalism has the added advantage of allowing compositionists to blame the past failure of writing instruction on mistaken epistemological assumptions and to predict greater success in the future. The fact that there appears to be a natural correspondence between anti-foundationalist thought and the process approach to composition, however, does not mean that such thought can provide a grounding for the practice of pedagogy, no matter how situational the pedagogical approach is; nor does a fully elaborated situational pedagogy depend on an understanding of or an appeal to anti-foundationalist thought.

To make this case, Fish argues that as a model of epistemology, anti-foundationalism could never yield instructions for achieving the epistemological state it seeks to describe. Coming to the realization that you are and always have been situated, embedded in a context, does not cause you to become better situated or more deeply embedded; this realization leaves you exactly where you were before the moment of realization—no better, and no worse. Even if you were to thoroughly and completely assimilate the knowledge that you and every practice, pedagogical or otherwise, is utterly context dependent—that is, even if you were to come to grasp this fact on a deep and self-conscious level—this knowledge would not allow you or your pedagogy to become more or better situated. To assert first that there is no knowledge independent of circumstantiality and then to propose that comprehending this fact will allow you to improve your circumstance and thus your knowledge is to have produced a circular argument: "Indeed, any claim in which the notion of situatedness is said to be a lever that allows us to get a purchase on situations is finally a claim to have escaped situatedness, and is therefore nothing more or less than a reinvention of foundationalism by the very form of thought that has supposedly reduced it to ruins" (348–49). In fact, this is exactly what happens in many of the works of composition theory that attempt to link anti-foundationalist thought with the revolution in composition instruction.[4]

In short, neither thoroughly assimilating anti-foundationalist thought nor teaching it to students will produce consequences in the world of praxis. While such thought might serve as a critique of pedagogical method, it cannot itself be employed as the justification of a pedagogical method—without, of course, thereby becoming foundationalist. Fish writes,

> To put the matter in a nutshell, the knowledge that one is in a situation has no particular payoff for any situation you happen to be in, because the constraints of that situation will not be relaxed by that knowledge. It follows, then, that teaching our students the lesson of anti-foundationalism, while it will put them in possession of a new philosophical perspective, will not give them a tool for operating in the world they already inhabit. Being told that you

are in a situation will help you neither to dwell in it more perfectly
nor to *write* within it more successfully. (351)

Despite the fervent desires of the many scholars and teachers in rhetoric
and composition who have embraced anti-foundationalist thought and
have sought to employ it in the service of a reformed writing pedagogy,
such efforts are futile.

Of course, someone might suggest that while we cannot employ anti-
foundationalist thought to govern or reform composition pedagogy, it
might be useful as an avenue to new and effective pedagogies. In other
words, perhaps the solution is to weaken the link between anti-
foundationalist thought and composition pedagogy. For example, if all
knowledge is situational, then this fact should lead compositionists to
"teach situations"—as many now attempt to do following exactly this line
of thought.[5] The trouble with the advice that composition instructors now
teach situations is that they cannot help but follow such advice in the weak
sense, and it is impossible to follow it in the strong sense. In the weak
sense, composition teachers are always already teaching situations because they are embedded in a context and because to require students to
direct a piece of writing toward a particular audience and for a particular
purpose is by definition to teach situations; such advice can't be followed
in the strong sense in that it would amount to teaching situations as if they
were "a new kind of object to which we could now turn our attention" and
as if we could "achieve a distance from them such that our accounts of
them would be a form of 'true' knowledge." However, both of these "as
ifs," says Fish, "once again reinvent foundationalism by substituting for
the discredited notion of determinate facts the finally indistinguishable
notion of determinate situations and by rendering unproblematic our
relationship to these newly determining entities" (351–52). Because a
situation is by definition always in flux, always in the act of becoming,
any attempt to fix it, to capture its essence, will necessarily fail because
it will only produce what it used to be, what it was at the moment of
capture. What's more, one can only attempt to fix or capture a situation
from within the situation itself; it is impossible to rise above the situation
in order to capture it. In a word, even weakening the connection between
anti-foundationalist thought and composition pedagogy will not pay off.

Fish comments that as a "card-carrying anti-foundationalist" he
would like to believe that the arguments he is committed to will have "a
beneficial effect on the teaching of writing," but such arguments simply
have no purchase in the world of praxis (347). The notion of situational,

context-bound knowledge is clearly too powerful to be threatened by a method that is unaware of its existence, and so foundationalist thought is in no position to *harm* composition research or pedagogy; similarly, embracing anti-foundationalist thought and teaching it to students will not enable compositionists to influence pedagogy, so anti-foundationalist thought is in no position to *improve* composition research or pedagogy. That is, both theory hope and theory fear are unwarranted. Theory, then, can have no consequences in the world of composition praxis.

The Emptiness of Principle

> I am tempted to turn this into an imperative—perhaps, with a nod to Fredric Jameson, "always politicize"—but the imperative would be unnecessary, for that is what we do all the time, whether we choose to or not.
> —Stanley Fish

> Taking sides, weapon in hand, is not a sign of zealotry or base partisanship; it is the sign of morality; and it is the morality of taking sides, of frank and vigorous political action, that is celebrated (not urged; it is inevitable) in the pages that follow.
> —Stanley Fish

To make his case against theory, Fish has drawn his examples primarily from literary criticism, but over time his anti-theory argument evolved to encompass any appeal to general principle, and to make this case he turned to issues arising from contemporary debates about liberal political philosophy, First Amendment rights, affirmative action policies, and multiculturalism. He develops his argument in *Doing What Comes Naturally* and *There's No Such Thing as Free Speech*, but *The Trouble with Principle* is perhaps the most sustained and cogent articulation of his position. As the title suggests, this book attempts to lay out the specifics of his anti-principle position. He rehearses the general outline of his argument in the book's Prologue, "Taking Sides."

Central to liberal political philosophy is the notion that a just society is based on such principles as "fairness," principles that supposedly exist in the abstract, independent of any specific situation or context. We are all urged to pledge allegiance not to specific persons or desired outcomes but to abstract norms that remain detached from and neutral toward particular persons and that are indifferent to outcomes. A high premium is put on such abstractions as fairness, impartiality, merit, mutual respect, neutrality, and reasonableness. Such abstractions are thought to be capable of being defined in ways that allow them to remain free from partisan agendas and, thus, are thought to be capable of serving as the foundation of legal and political policies that favor no one person or group in particular but that respect all people and groups in general. While such efforts are well intentioned, they are doomed to fail, in Fish's estimation:

> The problem is that any attempt to define one of these abstractions—to give it content—will always and necessarily proceed from the vantage point of some currently unexamined assumptions about the way life is or should be, and it is those assumptions, contestable in fact but at the moment not contested or even acknowledged, that will really be generating the conclusions that are supposedly being generated by the logic of principle. (3)

That is, whoever is attempting to define "fairness" or "mutual respect" or any other such principle will necessarily be doing so from a particular context, which includes one's personal system of values. It is impossible to rise above one's context in order to fill in the content of so-called neutral principles.

Fairness, for example, will be defined differently by different people, and this abstraction will not be intelligible unless and until it is anchored in a specific standpoint. One person may feel that fairness means admitting someone to college solely of the basis of test scores, whereas another may feel that fairness means also taking into account the fact that a student comes from a context of poverty and disadvantage. No definition of fairness exists independent of the kind of conditions or substance that must be supplied by necessarily interested parties (since all parties are necessarily interested). Once some kind of substance is supplied, however, neutral principles by definition lose their neutrality. That is, the oft-touted virtue of neutral principles is that they are supposedly devoid of substantive commitments; they purportedly afford a space within which "substantive agendas can make their case without prior advantage or disadvantage" (3). Yet, some substance *must* be supplied in order to make the principle—fairness, in this example—intelligible. Hence, there really is no such thing as a neutral principle; there is no such thing as a principle not already informed by the substantive content of the person appealing to the principle. While questions of fairness are central to intractable policy debates, invoking the principle of fairness will not advance these debates because at a certain level such debates are about "what fairness (or neutrality or impartiality) really is" (3). In effect, a contest over the content of a particular issue is also a contest over two or more contending notions of fairness (or impartiality or whatever principle is being invoked).

Even if it were possible to produce a general principle devoid of specific content—a notion of fairness, say, untethered to any specific perspective or ideological orientation—it would be of no use, says Fish, because it would by empty. That is, appealing to it would not point you in any specific direction in relation to other possible directions. Its very emptiness renders it useless as a moral compass. In effect, a neutral principle is a floating signifier, an "unoccupied vessel waiting to be filled by whoever gets to it first or with the most persuasive force" (7). In fact, it is exactly this condition of emptiness, its status as a floating signifier available for people to invest with substance, that makes neutral principles so politically useful—and even potentially dangerous, since they can be employed to further evil (as defined by you) ends just as easily as more positive (as defined by you) goals:

> It is because they don't have the constraining power claimed for them (they neither rule out nor mandate anything) and yet have the *name* of constraints (people think that when you invoke fairness you call for something determinate and determinable) that neutral principles can make an argument look as though it has a support higher or deeper than the support provided by its own substantive thrust. Indeed, the vocabulary of neutral principle can be used to disguise substance so that it appears to be the inevitable and nonengineered product of an impersonal logic. (4)

In other words, a general principle such as fairness is deployed as a weapon in political, legal, and ethical struggles precisely because it masks the interestedness of those appealing to it and cloaks the fact that the actual policy, law, or proposal being advanced in the name of the principle is embedded in specific historical circumstances and furthers the interests and objectives of one set of individuals over and against the interests and objectives of others.

The fact that general principles do not exist and the fact that they can be deployed to effect harm may seem at odds; however, there is no contradiction in declaring that, on the one hand, general principles do not exist (that is, that they have no substance except when they are invoked and thus invested with a particular substance that furthers a particular agenda) and that, on the other hand, they can be deployed to further odious agendas (that is, agendas that you yourself find to be odious). It is precisely the emptiness of principles (the fact that they can mean everything and thus nothing and therefore do not exist in any meaningful way *as neutral principles*) that makes them available to be used to do harmful (or good) work in the world. In other words, neutral principles do not exist as genuinely "neutral" principles independent of someone's agenda, but the vocabulary of neutrality causes principles to become very powerful tools in the political arena exactly because such language masks particular agendas. Fish writes, "The fact that the game of neutral principles is really a political game—the object of which is to package your agenda in a vocabulary everyone, or almost everyone, honors—is itself neutral and tells you nothing about how the game will be played in a particular instance" (7). For example, someone may very well invoke the principle of fairness (or some other principle), but the mere fact of invoking this terminology tells you nothing of whether you will or will not agree with the petitioner's agenda and with the petitioner's definition of fairness until you have heard the substance that he or she has packaged under the label "fair." Nothing about the word "fair" would alert you ahead of time as to where that person is likely to stand on the issue in question.

Fish maintains that it would not be unusual or inconsistent to attack the rhetoric of neutral principles in one instance and to employ that very same rhetoric in another, because in both instances what grounds a person's stance is his or her convictions and commitments, and "the means used to advance them would be secondary" (8). People typically begin with a strong conviction and then employ (or attack) a principle to advance that belief; they don't begin with a principle and then arrive at a strong conviction. If this modus operandi sounds like a description of Machiavellian "ends justify the means" conduct, it is indeed, but Fish is quick to stipulate that he is only reporting on how things work, not advocating that they ought to work that way. Because it is impossible to disentangle oneself from substantive agendas, ends-based behavior simply cannot be avoided. People will always seek to further their own agendas and to defeat those that they oppose. Fish is only pointing out "for the umpteenth time" that "when all is said and done there is nowhere to go except to the goals and desires that already possess you, and nothing to do but try as hard as you can to implement them in the world" (8–9).

Machiavelli, in fact, seems to have gotten things right. Fish points out that Machiavelli rails against the "idealizing language" of moral and political theory because it is "that high-sounding and pious vocabulary that gets in the way of understanding the only knowledge worth having, 'knowledge of the actions of men'" (qtd. in "Taking" 13). In Machiavelli's universe, one avenue to certain ruin is to contemplate imagined utopian states rather than the hard realities of the real world and to adhere to invariant rules while ignoring specific contexts, because such conduct would "sacrifice the values and interests at stake in a particular moment to a formal consistency that valued nothing but itself—the consistency, in short, of neutral principle" (14). Machiavelli has no respect for those who avoid taking sides in political struggles and who instead defer to neutral principles. "As a general thing," he writes in *The Prince*, "anyone who is not your friend will advise neutrality, while anyone who is your friend will ask you to join him, weapon in hand" (qtd. in "Taking" 14). Thus, Fish declares, far from being a sign of base zealotry, taking sides, defending and fighting for one's heartfelt convictions, is a sign of high morality.

Principle and the Politics of Difference

> As we have seen, there are principles aplenty—autonomy, respect, toleration, equality—but when they are put into play by sophisticated intelligences, the result is not resolution but a sharpened sense of the blind alleys into which they lead us.
>
> —Stanley Fish

> No one could possibly *be* a multiculturalist in any interesting and coherent sense.
>
> —Stanley Fish

The trouble with neutral principle is that while it can be employed as a political weapon in any number of debates, its disinterestedness is hardly ever questioned. For years, Fish has traced various ways in which scholars, politicians, judges, or interest groups have deployed the vocabulary of neutral principle in the service of particular political or legal ends. A representative example of his analysis of such vocabulary in a specific area of inquiry is his "Boutique Multiculturalism." In it, he attempts to unpack the complex and often contradictory claims of those who espouse some version of multiculturalism.

Fish distinguishes between two types of multiculturalism: "boutique" and "strong." Boutique multiculturalists exhibit a shallow or superficial flirtation with other cultures, as in patronizing ethnic restaurants, admiring a culture's art or music, and appreciating its distinct traditions. They are "boutique" multiculturalists in that they exoticize the culture of the other, turning it into a trendy object of their own pleasure, entertainment, and consumption. Their approval of another culture, however, will only extend to these surface manifestations of the culture; it will always cease when some core value, belief, or practice of the culture offends their personal notion of "decency," "fairness," or "civilized behavior." They might relish rap or gospel music, say, or eat soul food and attend exhibits of afrocentric art, but they would oppose affirmative action or an afrocentrist school curriculum. In other words, they resist or even oppose the culture "at precisely the point at which it matters most to its strongly committed members" (57). Boutique multiculturalists, then, will tolerate or even appreciate a culture—but only up to a certain point. The reason that they find no contradiction in expressing acceptance toward a culture and then withdrawing that acceptance once a central belief or practice of the culture conflicts with their own value system is that they posit an essential core of human nature and see outward differences—language, skin color, religious affiliation, or any other difference—as merely interesting variations on a theme; underneath these surface differences is the true core of humanity that we all allegedly share.

Boutique multiculturalists assume a universal human nature—a universal, trans-cultural human identity that is more fundamental than any specific manifestation of human identity colored by some particular cultural practice or attribute. What follows from this belief, says Fish, is that we all possess rights as human beings but not as members of certain classes—women or men, hispanics or caucasians, Jews or Christians—and while individuals are free to pursue their own practices, values, and beliefs, they can do so only up to the point at which a practice, value, or belief impedes, restricts, or interferes with the practices, values or beliefs of other individuals. For example, "One may choose either to read or to disdain pornography, but one who believes in pornography's liberatory effects cannot compel others to read it, and one who believes that pornography corrupts cannot forbid others to publish it." Yet, it is precisely these two actions, says Fish, "that pro- and antipornography forces will most want to take, since they flow logically from the beliefs of the respective parties and will be seen by those parties as positive moral requirements" (58). That is, boutique multiculturalists and the liberal rationalist tradition of which they are but one manifestation assume that an individual can and should bracket or set aside deeply held beliefs for the good of others (even when those deeply held convictions are central to the person's religion or entire belief system), and they in effect prescribe that the individual stop short of implementing those beliefs.

In contrast to boutique multiculturalists, strong multiculturalists value difference for its own sake, not as the surface sign of some more fundamental human nature. Rather than simply turning other cultures into the object of their own pleasure, entertainment, and consumption, strong multiculturalists are thoroughly committed to the flourishing of other cultures, and they actively seek to foster the unique distinctiveness of each culture and group.[6] Thus, they favor making special adjustments to help maintain the distinctiveness of other cultures or to right a discriminatory practice between groups, such as affirmative action laws and policies attempt to do. Rather than a superficial respect for other cultures, strong multiculturalists have a deep and abiding respect for all cultures and believe that every culture has a right to thrive and to assert its own unique identity. The first principle of the strong multiculturalist, then, is not rationality or some extra-cultural fundamental humanness but tolerance.

While at first glance strong multiculturalists may seem preferable to boutique multiculturalists, Fish believes that the only real difference between them is one of degree. The problem with basing one's multiculturalism on the principle of tolerance is that "you cannot possibly be faithful to it" because, as in the case of boutique multiculturalism, you will eventually find a practice, value, or belief in the culture that is central and intrinsic to that culture but that is repugnant to you and your own value system—a form of intolerance, say, at the very core of the culture and that helps define its distinctiveness:

> At this point, the strong multiculturalist faces a dilemma: either he stretches his toleration so that it extends to the intolerance residing at the heart of a culture he would honor, in which case tolerance is no longer his guiding principle, or he condemns the core intolerance of that culture (recoiling in horror when Khomeini calls for the death of Rushdie), in which case he is no longer according it respect at the point where its distinctiveness is most obviously at stake. (61)

Most strong multiculturalists, says Fish, will choose the latter course, thereby, in the end, revealing themselves *not* to be strong multiculturalists after all. In fact, he believes that when all is said and done strong multiculturalism is simply "a somewhat deeper instance of the shallow category of boutique multiculturalism" (61). Neither type of multiculturalist is truly able to come to terms with difference. Whereas boutique multiculturalists do not take difference seriously, reading the marks of difference as mere matters of lifestyle, strong multiculturalists take difference so seriously as a general principle that they "cannot take any particular difference seriously, cannot allow its imperatives their full realization in a political program, for their full realization would inevitably involve the suppression of difference" (62). Fish can only conclude, then, that there really is no such thing as a multiculturalist; we all are, and always have been, uniculturalists.

The discourse of multiculturalism with its reliance on the general principle of tolerance is simply not productive. Fish believes that we should change the terms of debate and focus instead on a more productive distinction: between multiculturalism as a philosophical problem and multiculturalism as a demographic fact. Thinking about multiculturalism as an abstract concept that we must either support or reject only leads us down blind alleys; remembering, instead, that it is a fact of demographics in contemporary U.S. society removes the discussion from the unproductive discourse of affirmation and rejection. That is, once we acknowledge the undisputed fact that U.S. society now comprises a multitude of distinct cultural traditions, coming out *against* or *in favor* of this sociological condition seems, to use Fish's adjective, "rather silly"; it would be tantamount to coming out *against* or *in favor* of history itself. He proposes shifting the focus from "solving conceptual puzzles" to the "defusing of potential crises." As Fish says, "We may never be able to reconcile the claims of difference and community in a satisfactory formula, but we may be able to figure out a way for *these* differences to occupy the civic and political space of *this* community without coming to blows" (63).

Invoking Charles Taylor's concept, "inspired adhoccery," Fish suggests that we abandon appeals to general principles like tolerance and a universal core humanness and that we instead attempt to solve each local problem locally, appealing to the specific conditions and contingencies arising from the problem's context. Rather than seek to apply some rule or principle to a particular cultural problem, we should regard each "situation-of-crisis" as "an opportunity for improvisation," understanding all along that such solutions will always be temporary and context specific—that is, ad hoc. Solving local problems locally means that different solutions will be called for in different contexts; no one, general solution will fit all problems. Hence, multiculturalism will necessarily be—and actually already is—many things, not some single belief or condition. As a result, "In some sectors multiculturalism will take care of itself; in others its problematic will hardly register; and in others it will be a 'problem' that must be confronted" (64). What it will *not* be, however (and what it never has been), is a general belief, philosophical quandary, or course of action that is identical in all places.

The fact is that the business and academic worlds have long recognized multiculturalism as a hard reality. In many cases, corporations have instituted hiring and promotion policies that are responsive to the growing diversity of U.S. society, and they have mandated sensitivity programs to reduce and eliminate racial and ethnic tensions in the workplace. Such programs are typically established not because they derive from some philosophical egalitarianism but because they constitute sound business practice. Similarly, multiculturalism is "a baseline condition" in the academic world. Fish writes,

> Indeed, in many facets of American life there is no multiculturalism issue despite the fact that it is endlessly debated by pundits who pronounce on the meaning of democracy, the content of universal rights, the nature of community, the primacy of the individual, and so on. These mind-numbing abstractions may be the official currency of academic discussion, but they do not point us to what is really at stake in the large social and economic dislocations to which they are an inadequate (and even irrelevant) response. In and of themselves, they do no genuine work and insofar as they do any work it is in the service of the adhoccery to which they are rhetorically opposed. (65)

Despite the endless and pointless philosophizing of academics, despite all attempts to undergird it with grand principles of tolerance and democracy, multiculturalism is a fact of life in U.S. society, and the most productive response is to acknowledge its existence and to deal with any "problems" in their specific contexts. In fact, says Fish, that's all we can ever really do anyway, even when the issues are framed in the language of universal principle.

The urge to formulate universal principles such as tolerance to serve as a ground for a democratic social and political system is central to liberal thought, and Fish has argued against such thought for most of his career—not because he is persuaded by conservative ideology (he is not) but because he sees liberalism as ineffectual, and even silly.[7] Liberal political theorists, for instance, will often call for a civil society that is character-ized by "mutual respect" of even the most "fundamental differences," but such language always deconstructs itself. Fish contends that it is impos-sible to "respect" differences that are genuinely fundamental without disrespecting your own beliefs. Someone who strongly believes that abortion is infanticide could not "respect" the belief that abortions should be readily available to anyone who wants one and that taxpayer dollars can even be used to subsidize the procedure. In order to respect such a belief, you would have to set aside your deeply held convictions about the beginning of human life (and the legitimate use of public funds) and accept or at least tolerate behavior that you deem to be murder; and you would do this all in the name of a philosophical principle: tolerance, or mutual respect of fundamental differences. Besides, says Fish, you don't show respect for a view that you despise by tolerating it; you show true respect by taking it so seriously that you seek to defeat it.

Nevertheless, liberals, many in the tradition of Jürgen Habermas, envision a society in which bloodshed, and indeed conflict of any type, can be eliminated because all differences can be discussed reasonably and rationally, and appropriate solutions can be negotiated—or, if need be, arbitrated. Thus, liberal theorists overinvest in a model of public dis-course as genteel discussion, "civilized" conversation. It is as if, quips Fish, liberals—especially academic liberals—espouse a "world-as-phi-losophy-seminar" model of public discourse, where all disputes between "rational" people can be talked through and eventually resolved. Most versions of this model, however, exclude a priori those who are deemed to be *not* rational, *not* reasonable—fanatics, fundamentalists, those disrespectful of others' fundamental beliefs, for example—so rather than radical openness, this model exhibits its own insularity and exclusivity. Who may and may not sit at the seminar table is decided in advance by "rational" assessment of who is worthy, who is respect-ful enough, who is sufficiently reasonable. Rather than condemn the liberal model of public discourse for not living up to its advertised openness, however, Fish faults it for being too open. The desire to be open in the first place is what blinds liberals to the true extent and depth of the evil they oppose. The only way to defeat evil (or a misguided policy, or a harmful law, or a retrograde practice) is exactly that: to defeat it, not to try to persuade it from continuing to be evil. Fish adds,

> If you wish to strike a blow against beliefs you think pernicious, you will have to do something more than exclaim, "I exclude you from my community of mutual respect." That kind of exclusion will be no blow to an agenda whose proponents are not interested in being respected but in triumphing. Banishing hate speakers from your little conversation leaves them all the freer to pursue their deadly work in the dark corners from which you have averted your fastidious eyes. (69)

Thus, the liberal propensity to advance rational conversation as the premier method of conflict management is self-defeating. If the intent truly is to defeat an objectionable policy, law, or practice, then persuasion is the *least* likely way to accomplish this goal, and a false openness is counterproductive. Much better to confront one's opponent head on.

Liberalism's great mistake is that it cleaves to a naive faith in tolerance, persuasion, rationality, and the essential reasonableness and goodness of human nature. Such an agenda will never be capable of achieving victory in the hard cruel world. If liberals genuinely wish to thwart a policy, law, practice, or viewpoint that they find reprehensible, they will need to use the very techniques that liberalism repudiates: "acts of ungenerosity, intolerance, perhaps even repression" (69). That is, the only effective way to respond to evil is *not* to tolerate it but to contrive ways to extirpate it, to engage in the very kinds of acts that it has summarily ruled inappropriate and uncivil. But, says Fish,

> This is a lesson liberalism will never learn; it is the lesson liberalism is *pledged* never to learn because underlying liberal thought is the assumption that, given world enough and time (and so long as embarrassing "outlaws" have been discounted in advance), difference and conflict can always be resolved by rational deliberation, where rational deliberation is meant the kind of deliberation routinely engaged in by one's circle of friends. (69)[8]

The trouble with the liberal appeal to universal principles such as tolerance and mutual respect is that it transports people out of the rough-

and-tumble world of realpolitik and into a fantasy world disconnected from high-stakes struggles over concrete outcomes.

One example of how the liberal preoccupation with rational debate and universal principles prevents liberals from achieving their own goals is the dispute over hate speech. Liberals tend to think that there is some objective standard for identifying hate speech and that uttering such speech is a sign of ignorance or irrationality. The debate, then, is framed as one between the rational (deciding not to utter speech that is clearly hurtful to others) and the irrational (purposely uttering speech that is hateful or being unaware of the fact that such speech is hateful). The producers of hate speech, however, do not accept the judgment that their speech is hateful; they believe their speech to be *true*. Thus, far from a struggle between the rational and the irrational—as the liberals characterize it—this is really a clash between two opposing rationalities, "each of which is equally, but differently, intolerant" (70). Because there is no independent norm for designating an utterance as hateful (since what is "hateful" to some may simply be "true" to others), there in effect really is no such thing as hate speech.[9] That is, no utterance, no matter how offensive to some, will be universally offensive to everyone. And an utterance that seems perfectly neutral and benign to you (and to most others) could very well sound hateful to someone else. Thus, hate speech is not a "limitable category"; there is no way to define it so as to make it meet everyone's definition. If hate speech really cannot be satisfactorily defined, if no utterance will be clearly hateful to everyone and every utterance has the potential to be hateful to someone, then "hate speech" cannot be said to exist in any meaningful sense—that is, as a *general* category. Consequently, hate speech and rationality are not *generally* opposed, as the liberals contend; hate speech is "always at once someone's rationality and someone else's abomination" (70).

The fact that hate speech and rationality are not *generally* opposed means that hate speech—that is, speech hateful to some—is rational, not, as liberals suggest, a clear case of the irrational. By dubbing hate speech "irrational," liberals thrust it into the realm of social "problem." Labeling hate speech a problem seems to suggest that it is susceptible to "correction," perhaps through education, dialogue, or censure. It takes on the form of social disease that can be cured. But since hate speech in fact belongs to the realm of the rational, labeling it a problem that can be remedied through rational means (education, dialogue, or shame) is misguided. Fish suggests that the time has come to stop characterizing hate speech as a problem arising from irrational convictions and instead to think of it as the words of your enemy:

> Everything changes, however, once hate speech is seen not as evidence of some cognitive confusion or as a moral anomaly but as the expression of a morality you despise, that is, as what your enemy (not the universal enemy) says. If you think of hate speech as evidence of moral or cognitive confusion, you will try to clean the confusion up by the application of good reasons; but if you think that hate speakers, rather than being confused, are simply wrong—they reason well enough but their reasons are anchored in beliefs (about racial characteristics, sexual norms, and so on) you abhor—you will not place your faith in argument but look for something stronger. (70–71)

The advantage of conceiving hate speech as the words of your enemy rather than as a deficit in someone's reasoning is that you stand a much better chance of finding ways to prevent or curtail it *in specific contexts*. After all, how likely is it that a racist or homophobe will be swayed by a tidy logical argument to abandon his or her heartfelt convictions about race or sexuality? You may very well convince a racist to stop uttering racist epithets in your presence, but you are not likely to persuade the person to become anti-racist.[10]

In other words, if you understand hate speech to be a social problem, you will seek to rectify it through some therapy; however, if you understand it to be the words of your enemy, you will seek to devise a strategy to inhibit its growth. Once you understand hate speech to be the words of your enemy, the heuristic for evaluating the effectiveness of a response to instances of such speech will change: you will no longer ask, "Will it eliminate the pathology?" You will ask instead, "Will it retard the growth of the evil I loathe and fear?" (71).

The problem with the traditional approach to hate speech is that liberals, appealing to universal principles to guide their actions (especially tolerance and mutual respect), have assumed that hate speech itself is a universal, something that transcends context and that is universally recognizable; they imagine that it can be remedied through yet another assumed universal: human rationality. Transporting hate speech into the netherlands of such abstraction assures defeat.[11] Racism will not be eradicated through dialogue; the best we can hope for is "a succession of tactical victories in which the enemy is weakened, discomforted, embarrassed, deprived of political power, and on occasion routed" (71). Thus, the most effective way to address questions of multiculturalism and other favorite liberal causes such as the eradication of hate speech is to become radically contextual, to approach each individual instance or "problem" within the specific constraints of the situation at hand. Again, it means solving local problems locally, devising different solutions for different contexts because no one, general solution will fit all problems.

Fish's argument against the appeal to principle is a cousin to his argument against the appeal to theory, in that the appeal to theory, both in literary criticism as well as in other disciplines, is a project that seeks to establish universal rules that regulate a particular practice. Both appeals are efforts to set aside all personal bias and self-interest in order to discern and then codify the rules by which something works—literary interpretation, culture, hate speech, and so on. Both appeals constitute efforts to guide practice from a position above and outside the practice. Both are attempts to reform practice by neutralizing self-interest, by substituting for one's personal perspective a general rationality. Both assume that at the end of the day, rationality will always prevail. And when all is said and done, neither can have any true consequence in the world of practice.

Chapter 3

The Story of Rhetoric: Constructing the Ground
Upon Which You Confidently Walk

If anything can be said to unite Fish's interventions in so many disparate areas of inquiry it is his belief in the centrality of rhetoric. Whether he is discussing how disciplines conduct their work, how political positions triumph, or how practice always derives from specific situations despite the grandiose theories employed to justify them, he consistently turns to the specific local, contingent context—to the rhetorical situation at play—to explain how something works. When he contends that a theory will not substantively affect the practice it seeks to elucidate, inform, or improve, he is saying that people fashion their practices within the specific constraints of the rhetorical situations they find themselves in. When he asserts that composition instructors have no choice *but* to teach situations and that they will not be able to reform writing pedagogy by appealing to theory, he is observing that they are always already located within rhetorical situations and that the very act of directing students to write to a particular audience for a particular purpose is precisely to engage themselves and their students in rhetoric. When he declares that a general principle such as fairness can be deployed as a weapon in political, legal, and ethical struggles to further the interests and objectives of one set of individuals over and against the interests and objectives of others, he is simply describing how agents operate rhetorically to achieve their ends. When he argues that despite all attempts to undergird multiculturalism with grand principles of tolerance and democracy, multiculturalism is a fact of life and the most productive response is to deal with any "problems" in their specific contexts (and that that's all we can ever really do anyway), he is insisting that all we can ever do is operate rhetorically within the specific situations that present themselves to us. As he says in the interview in chapter 5, rhetoric is the "necessary center," and "substantial realities are products of rhetorical, persuasive, political efforts." In fact, his insistence on the centrality of rhetoric is what led him to embrace Roger Kimball's description of him as "the contemporary sophist"—an epithet that Kimball intended to be derogatory but that Fish adopts with pride. An excellent example of Fish's description of how rhetoric works is his analysis of the intricacies of legal discourse.

Rhetoric and Interpretation in Legal Discourse

> It need hardly be said that I am not the first to declare that the operations of law are rhetorical.
>
> —Stanley Fish

> It follows, then, that whenever there is a dispute about the plain meaning of a contract, at some level the dispute is between two (or more) visions of what life is or should be like.
>
> —Stanley Fish

Given the zest and vitality with which Fish writes about legal discourse, one is tempted to conclude that he enjoys writing about the law more than any other subject. He certainly seems to derive substantial satisfaction from such efforts, as evidenced by his spirited and witty treatments of subjects legal. A representative example of one of his interventions into ongoing discussions about the operations of legal discourse is "The Law Wishes to Have Formal Existence." The title signifies two desires of or self-imposed pressures on the law: it desires to remain distinct from other (nonlegal) endeavors and thus avoids being assimilated into or subordinated to other concerns and undertakings; and as a distinct endeavor it desires to maintain its autonomy and thus avoids appealing to some supplementary discourse to help specify what the law is and how it should operate (otherwise it would lose both its autonomy and its distinctness). Historically, the two most persistent threats to the law's autonomy have been morality and interpretation. While the law wishes to maintain a relationship with morality—to be able to declare that its rules and decisions correspond somewhat to the values and behavior generally thought to be morally right rather than always conflicting with those values and behavior—it avoids meshing perfectly with moral institutions because the law then would in effect be superfluous (as is arguably the case with the Taliban in Afghanistan). That is, if the institution of law and the institutions of religion were to correspond perfectly, then citizens would be able to extrapolate from moral precepts exactly what their legal obligations are in any given situation, thus rendering the institution of law redundant.[1] Interpretation is seen as a threat to the law in that it is characterized as the act of disregarding or dismissing the meaning inherent in a text in favor of another more partisan or interested reading of the text. Both morality and interpretation, then, threaten to substitute local or individual concerns, values, or readings (since there are multiple moralities and potential readings) for the larger, more stable, supposedly disinterested perspective of the law.

The law attempts to keep partisanship in check by appealing to the doctrine of formalism, the belief that it is possible to compose language with such precision that a text's meaning will always be clear and understandable despite the individual perspectives of those reading the text. Formalists assume that statutes, contracts, and other legal documents can be written in such a way as to prescribe that agents take or not take certain actions under specific circumstances—regardless of the agents' desires, ethical creeds, political convictions, or personal values—and that it will always be clear precisely when, why, and under what conditions such actions should be taken. Once a statement is expressed in its *proper form* as a legal statement or question, this text will generate a chain of circumscribed actions unaffected by personal agendas. In other words, the very form of legal discourse allows the law to adjudicate fairly and independently between two or more contending interests while establishing standards that claim to rise above any specific interests.

Fish, of course, insists that no such independent position is possible, that individual desires, ethical creeds, political convictions, and personal values are always already at play in the production and consumption of legal texts. The aura of blind objectivity that the legal system embraces as its identity is an illusion—indeed, an impossibility. He argues that although the law yearns to have a formal existence, such aspirations will consistently be frustrated because interpretation will always play a role in any specification of what the law is, and thus any such specification will be susceptible to challenge. Rather than concluding, however, that the law completely fails to have formal existence, he claims that in a very important sense it "always succeeds, although the nature of that success—it is a political/rhetorical achievement—renders it bitter to the formalist taste" (144). Fish in effect redescribes how formalism operates within legal discourse.

To make this case, he turns to contract law, where often issues are resolved by appealing to what a contract "expressly" says and does not say. In the very act of proclaiming that a document exhibits undisputed meaning, a party will tend to flesh out the language that he or she is in the process of asserting is already immediately clear. That is, the party will appeal to the plain meaning of a text and then begin to supply language to stabilize the meaning that supposedly already is stable. Thus, rather than simply reproducing what is there in the text for everyone to see, the party will produce a "reading" of that text—an interpretation. And, of course, the opposing party will be engaging in exactly the same behavior. So, rather than such cases being instances of what a contract clearly provides and one side's attempt to bend the language to fit a meaning not expressly stated in the text, they are inevitably instances of two (or more) sides constructing the language to fit meanings that they then will assert are expressly stated in the text. If the meaning of a document truly could be self-evident, then no explanation would ever be necessary; indeed, explanation would be superfluous. Yet, no document simply declares its own meaning; explanation, interpretation will invariably be required.

To illustrate, Fish discusses trade usage cases. *Trade usage* refers to the specific language and conventions of meaning used by the members of a particular trade, as distinct from *ordinary usage*, the conventional meanings of words as people use them in their everyday contexts. In most trade usage cases, one party attempts to demonstrate that a contract's words do not mean what they appear to mean because they should be read within the specialized context of the trade's usage, a context defined by the parties' expectations. He cites one case about a dispute over a delivery schedule, for example, in which the court ruled that the term "June–August" could be construed as excluding delivery in August, and he cites another in which the court ruled that a contract to provide a shipment of steel measuring thirty-six inches was satisfied by a delivery of thirty-seven-inch steel. He points out that if in "certain persuasively established circumstances" the term "June–August" can be understood to exclude August, and if "thirty-six" can be interpreted as meaning thirty-seven, "then anything, once a sufficiently elaborated argument is in place, can mean anything: 'thirty-six' could mean seventy-five, or, in relation to a code so firmly established that it governed the expectations of the parties, 'thirty-six' could mean detonate the atomic bomb" (148). That is, such readings of contract language have less to do with demonstrating "formal congruity" than with exercising rhetorical prowess:

> As long as one party can tell a story sufficiently overarching so as to allow the terms of the contract and the evidence of trade usage to fit comfortably within its frame, that evidence will be found consistent rather than contradictory. What is and is not a "reasonable construal" will be a function of the persuasiveness of the construer and not of any formal fact that is perspicuous before some act of persuasion has been performed. (149)

A dispute over the language of a contract, then, is a *rhetorical* contest, a struggle over whose narrative of "the facts" is most convincing to those in a position to rule on the dispute's resolution.

Some legal mechanisms attempt to prevent the seepage of interpretation into the process of adjudicating disputes over contractual language. The "parol evidence rule," for example, stipulates that evidence extrinsic to a case may not be introduced in order to interpret, alter, or supplement the terms of a contract. Yet, despite this rule, the court has allowed such evidence under certain conditions. In fact, it is not uncommon in contract law to argue that because a given contract could not possibly include every piece of information potentially germane to a particular matter, it necessarily will remain silent on some relevant issues; consequently, information extrinsic to the contract might be introduced to help clarify important issues. But as Fish points out, the number of things that any given contract is silent on is limitless, and so there is "no end to the information that can be introduced if it can be linked narratively to a document" (150). Thus, despite formal mechanisms (such as the parol evidence rule) crafted to prevent interpretation from eroding the supposedly express language of contracts and statutes, a dispute over the language of a contract will always be a *rhetorical* contest, a rivalry between two or more competing narratives about the facts of the case.

Notwithstanding the parol evidence rule and other efforts by formalists to eliminate interpretation from the legal process, a contract will always be subject to interpretation. No contract can be so well crafted as to "resist incorporation into a persuasively told story in the course of whose unfolding its significance may be altered from what it had seemed to be" (151). However, rather than concluding from this fact that the parol evidence rule is worthless or powerless, Fish concludes that the rule in fact functions exactly as it should. Even though numerous cases demonstrate that parties have constructed stories that have successfully thwarted the parol evidence rule, those same cases make clear that a party cannot simply tell "any old story"; the story "must be one that fashions its coherence out of materials that it is required to take into account" (151). The important fact is not that a given case might have circumvented the parol evidence rule but that it is precisely the parol evidence rule that it felt obliged to circumvent. Fish explains,

> In short, the parol evidence rule is of more service to the law's wish to have a formal existence than one might think from these examples. The service it provides, however, is not (as is sometimes claimed) the service of safeguarding a formalism already in place, but the weaker (although more exacting) service of laying down the route by which a formalism can be fashioned. I am aware, of course, that this notion of the formal will seem strange to those for whom a formalism is what is "given" as opposed to something that is made. But, in fact, efficacious formalisms—marks and sounds that declare meanings to which all relevant parties attest—are always the product of the forces—desire, will, intentions, circumstances, interpretation—they are meant to hold in check. (152)

Despite the intention of those who attempt to strip interpretation from the legal process, reading a contract or statute will always be exactly that— a reading, a matter of interpretation, and also a matter of rhetoric, of constructing the most persuasive rendering of that reading.

The parol evidence rule, then, functions in two stages. First, it places constraints on the interpretation a party can make and thus constrains the narrative the party may construct; that is, it allows certain avenues of interpretation given the facts and circumstances of a case but not others. Because it places restrictions on the kind and extent of the interpretation of the contract's supposedly plain and clear language, it in effect restricts the kind and extent of the narrative of those facts that the party can then produce. Once a party has devised a persuasive narrative, the parol evidence rule then serves to protect the meanings that issue from that narrative, in effect saying, "You must not disregard this meaning—that is, the meaning that has been established in the course of the interpretive process—for one that has not been so established" (153).

When Fish observes that the outcome of such cases depends on the relative persuasiveness of contesting narratives of the facts, he does not mean simply the logic of the arguments being put forth. Persuasiveness in this context—indeed, in all contexts—is a product of the relationship between the arguments and one's (often tacit) beliefs. In fact, much of the work of persuasion (and thus of specifying what is "clear" and "plain" in the first place) derives from this layer of convictions that are so submerged that they in large part determine what will qualify as an argument and what will qualify as persuasive. Thus, an individual's beliefs—which, of course, include moral dispositions—will play a substantial if often invisible role in both fashioning and in receiving a "persuasive" narrative. If people's notions of what will and will not constitute a persuasive argument issue in part from their heartfelt convictions—beliefs that also include moral dispositions—then any dispute over the content of a contract is also at a certain level a contest over two or more competing conceptions of what life or society should be. Not only is it impossible to rise above or outside of one's convictions, those convictions are the very lens through which the world is viewed.

In short, the law operates not by choosing between a literal meaning and a contextual reading; rather, it weighs two or more relatively (relative to one another) persuasive narratives that arise from competing contexts and ideological perspectives. As a result, the law is continually in a process of self-creation, perpetually creating and re-creating itself from the very forces—agents' desires, ethical creeds, political convictions, personal values, and ideological perspectives—that it is pledged to reject. While some observers have described this process as a farce or as a tragedy, arguing that it only demonstrates the failure of the legal system and the collapse of justice, Fish insists that it demonstrates the exact opposite—that it is "a signal example of the way in which human beings are able to construct the roadway on which they are traveling, even to the extent of 'demonstrating' in the course of building it that it was there all the while" (156). Far from a failure, the history of the construction and application of legal doctrine is a success because the system keeps moving forward despite daily assaults on it from immensely complex social, political, economic, and ideological "urgencies." It confronts each challenge within the context of its particular urgencies—that is, rhetorically—and fashions decisions (and, thus, itself) in each instance from those urgencies. The fact that the law operates rhetorically rather than mechanically from neutral principles stripped of human contingencies does not signify its failure; it signifies its triumph, in that it is responsive to those human contingencies. In actuality, the law has no choice; it cannot proceed in any other way than rhetorically, despite all attempts to prevent it from doing so.

Notwithstanding the efforts of the formalists, then, interpretation is always already a part of legal decision making. The same is true with the other perceived threat to the law: morality. Just as formalists have crafted mechanisms such as the parol evidence rule to prevent interpretation from eroding the law's presumed integrity and objectivity, so too have they devised mechanisms that seek to prevent morality from chipping away at the law's independence. One such mechanism is the doctrine of consideration. Anyone who has taken even the most basic contract law course understands that a contract is not legally enforceable if it does not include consideration—that is, if a party does not receive *something* (anything, really) in return for whatever good or service that person is providing. To constitute a legal contract, that contract must specify that each party to the agreement will receive something of value. This requirement was created in order to separate legal from moral obligations, in that it provides a formal criterion by which parties may bind themselves rather than a subjective, moral criterion; that is, the law does not enter the more subjective realm of determining exactly how much compensation is "fair" or "equitable" and instead simply lays out the shape or form that a legally binding contract should take. In effect, consideration is a device that seeks to detach a legal agreement from its specific context so that it will rise above or stand outside that context. Were a court to attempt to ascertain whether consideration in a case is equitable or just, it would be operating in the hazy, value-laden world of the moral—the very domain that the doctrine of consideration was created to bar the law from entering. Barred from the murky world of the moral, the law is assured of conducting its business in the much clearer sphere of the rational—or so the formalists believe.

The intent of the doctrine of consideration is identical to that of the parol evidence rule: to disengage the law from the specific and variable contexts of the parties to an agreement so that no one party can create a new and different contract from the one that existed prior to a dispute. In the same way that it is impossible to detach interpretation from the "reading" of the supposedly plain and clear language of a contract, it is impossible to sever one's particular moral perspective from that reading. Or, stated more accurately, every interpretation arises from one's particular moral perspective; there simply is no such thing as a reading disconnected from one's perspective and values. In fact, Fish argues that rather than constituting separate threats to the law's autonomy and integrity, interpretation and morality constitute the exact same threat, in that interpretation is "the name for the activity by which a particular moral vision makes its hegemonic way into places from which it has been formally barred" (158).

The history of contract law, then, is not a story of the successful exclusion of morality from its precincts; rather, it is one in which a particular morality has won the day: the "very embodiment" of market morality, a morality of "arm's length dealing between agents without histories, gender, or class affiliations" (159). This one version of morality has become so firmly ensconced that it is no longer perceived to be a particular perspective (it is seen as "mere procedure"), and its protective procedures (such as the doctrine of consideration) are no longer recognized for what they are: attempts to "keep the other moralities at bay." Fish writes, "Just as the winning interpretation of a contract must persuade the court that it is not an interpretation at all but a plain and clear meaning, so the winning morality must persuade the court (or direct the court in the ways of persuading itself) that it is not a morality at all but a perspicuous instance of fidelity to the law's form" (159). A dispute over the terms of a contract is not only a contest over competing narratives of the facts of the case but also a struggle between two ways of seeing the world, and these contests must take place by appealing to the formal language of the law and by thus appearing to fit within its purview—that is, they must operate rhetorically.

In the same way that parties to a contract will construct a narrative of the facts but are constrained by the parol evidence rule from concocting just any old narrative, parties will insinuate their moral perspectives into the law but are constrained by the doctrine of consideration from doing so in any old form; rather, those perspectives "must be worked into a form that matches the picture of consideration, the picture of a freely chosen giving up of something in return for something just as freely proffered" (162). Thus, the doctrine continues to do its work—constrain the actions of parties—but just not in the same way that formalists think it does. What's more, the fact that contract law stipulates that it must remain above specific contexts, interpretations, and moralities but then embraces those very same specific contexts, interpretations, and moralities is not a fatal inconsistency; it is simply how the law must function. Contract law endorses a view of legal transaction in which the features of transaction are purely formal so as to maintain its autonomy and independence; yet, at the same time, it attempts to be "sensitive to our always changing intuitions about how people ought to behave" and so it continually smuggles in the very forces it claims to exclude (163). This modus operendi is less an inconsistency than an operational necessity because legal obligation was never "formal" in the first place; it always was and will continue to be the extension of a particular social perspective.

Fish is not alone in pointing out these seeming inconsistencies in how the law works. Many critical legal studies scholars, for example, complain that the fact that the law operates rhetorically despite its formal veneer means that what really works in the legal system is whatever someone can get away with. They argue that the legal system is bankrupt because it is incapable of producing consistent outcomes that flow logically from the formal rules, doctrines, and procedures of the law. Legal decisions too often appear to be ad hoc, the products of mere rhetorical manipulation on the part of interested parties. What's more, because the law conceals its ad hoc operations in the language of objectivity, formalism, and disinterestedness, it is blatantly deceitful and thus not worthy of the public trust. The mythological figure of blind Justice dispassionately weighing the facts is exactly that—mere myth, a grand story that cloaks the messy, partisan contention that characterizes how the law really works.

Although Fish's analysis and the critiques of the legal system put forward by critical legal studies proponents share many aspects in common, Fish arrives at very different conclusions. He does not conclude that the ad hoc, rhetorical nature of legal discourse demonstrates that the law is bankrupt or deceitful or unworthy of the public trust—quite the opposite. Legal discourse is not philosophical discourse; both traditions have different standards of consistency. Unlike philosophy (at least certain schools), the law is pragmatic; it is dependent on judging evidence in specific situations:

> A rhetorical jurisprudence does not ask timeless questions; it inquires into the local conditions of persuasion, into the reasons that *work;* and what it finds interesting about the law's normative claims is not whether or not they can be cashed (in strict terms they cannot), but the leverage one can achieve by invoking them. (171)

From a pragmatic perspective, the inconsistency of legal doctrine is exactly what enables the law to work because it is only within specific contexts that arguments weigh or fail to weigh the evidence and thus prevail or fail to prevail. The rhetorical nature of the law is only a liability or weakness if one expects the law to function algorithmically, mechanically meting out decisions with no real cognizance of or sensitivity to the real human circumstances involved—and no one, especially the critical legal studies proponents, advocates that. In short, what many decry as the law's greatest weakness, Fish sees as its strength.

The story of legal discourse, then, is "the story of rhetoric, the art of constructing the (verbal) ground upon which you then confidently walk" (170). No other available alternative way of operating is acceptable—or, in reality, possible. The determinate rationality of formalism is an impossibility, and the critical legal studies project of continually exposing the law's rhetoricity will not result in a change in the way the law conducts its business, though such constant critique may well succeed in retarding the progress of its business. But Fish doubts that perpetual critique will even have *that* consequence because "the law's creative rhetoricity will survive every effort to deconstruct it" (171). Rather than perceiving the law's rhetoricity to be a liability, Fish suggests that we recognize, appreciate, and even marvel at how complex, intricate, and effective the law is precisely because it is rhetorical and not mechanical.

The primary objective of many critical legal studies proponents is not to replace the U.S. system of jurisprudence with another, but to strengthen and improve this system by foregrounding its rhetorical nature. The assumption is that once all participants are fully aware that the law is rhetorical, they will be able to function more effectively (and ethically) within its precincts. Fish argues that such self-awareness presumes that somehow the participants can rise above the very rhetoricity that they are operating within. Understanding that legal discourse is rhetorical cannot serve to improve it unless participants could somehow be dislodged from that rhetoricity—which, of course, is impossible. Knowing that legal discourse is a system in which participants justify their actions rhetorically does not allow someone to achieve distance from those reasons or to be more (or less) persuaded by them. Fish writes,

> The lesson of the law's rhetoricity—the lesson that reasons are reasons only within the configurations of practice and are not reasons that generate practice from a position above it—must be extended to itself. It can no more serve as a master thesis than the formalist theses it replaces. Formalists at least make their mistake legitimately, since it is *their* position that local practices follow or should follow from master principles; it cannot, without internal contradiction, be a rhetorician's position, even when the master principle is rhetoric itself. (172)

The effort to establish rhetoric as a master category is yet another attempt to elucidate, inform, or improve practice from a position outside of that practice, outside the specific constraints of the rhetorical situations participants find themselves in—it is to forget that they are always already located within those rhetorical situations and cannot step outside of them.

Nevertheless, many critical legal studies scholars do in fact seek to establish rhetoric as a master category in an effort to reform legal practice. Some even go so far as to pronounce that lawyers and judges should always keep in mind as they practice the law the kind of society they ideally aspire to actualize.[2] While keeping in mind the kind of society humanity should aspire to achieve may in fact be a noble endeavor, it is not part of the customary business of the law as it is practiced. Lawyers and judges are in the business of arguing and evaluating *legal* questions, questions that directly pertain to a particular case at hand; the law is rooted in the very specific contexts of particular disputes over particular actions taken or not taken at particular points in time. Interrupting a discussion rooted in such specific circumstances in order to embark on a philosophical exploration of society's values and aspirations is to stop practicing law and to practice instead moral philosophy. If a judge, for example, were to interrupt the course of a case to philosophize about society's values, that judge would not be fulfilling his or her professional obligations as a judge—unless, of course, the philosophizing happened to be a prelude to announcing a ruling that flowed from the facts and arguments of the case. Those who call for lawyers and judges to keep in mind the kind of society they should aspire to are making a crucial mistake: they are conflating "the perspective from which one might ask questions about the nature of law (is it formal or moral or rhetorical?) with the perspective from which one might ask questions in the hope that the answers will be of use in getting on with a legal job of work" (173). The first perspective is one of metacritical inquiry and will have no bearing on the outcome of a case; the second perspective is one in which legal decisions can logically flow.[3]

Some critical legal studies proponents espouse a form of critical self-consciousness similar to that promoted by anti-foundationalists in cultural studies and other fields. They believe that becoming cognizant of the law's rhetoricity and keeping that awareness at the forefront of one's consciousness will cause legal actors to become more aware of their own tacit assumptions and more open to other perspectives; such self-reflexivity will ideally lead them to an appreciation of the limitations of their own parochial perspectives and to an increased recognition of the multiple perspectives and positions at play in a discourse. Some versions of critical self-consciousness even posit that conflict will diminish and become much less frequent as critical self-consciousness becomes more widespread. In such a vision, the need for persuasion will eventually disappear because society will have become more "rational." In effect, this is a Habermasian vision of a rational and harmonious society in which "all parties will lay down their forensic arms and join together in the effort to build a new and more rational community" (174). Needless to say, Fish finds such fantasizing to be disconnected from reality. As he has argued in numerous venues, there simply is no such thing as critical self-consciousness, in that being critically aware in the way that it is typically described would necessarily entail simultaneously understanding that one is embedded in ideology and somehow mentally floating free of that embeddedness; and this is inconceivable, an unattainable state. It is equally inconceivable that individuals would—or even could—abandon their heartfelt convictions for some abstract egalitarianism. In short, being aware that the law is rhetorical and keeping that awareness at the forefront of one's consciousness will have no consequence in the world of legal practice, much less in society in general.

While metacritical analysis of how the law works and how it came to work the way it does may be interesting and even useful in certain intellectual contexts, such analysis and the knowledge generated by it does not affect the practice of law because it is a *different* endeavor. If the law were to "deploy its categories and concepts in the company of an analysis of their roots in extralegal discourses, it would not be exercising, but dismantling its authority; in short, it would no longer be law" (176). A critical or sociological or deconstructive analysis of the law may well need to foreground how the law is based on the appropriation of other discourses, but in order to *practice* law this knowledge must be repressed. That is, the law in effect must undergo a kind of "forgetfulness"; it must repress awareness of its debts and complicities, otherwise it would be unable to function. In order to function, the law must single-mindedly keep its attention on the specifics of the case at hand and not be distracted by metacritical or extralegal factors. In fact, Fish claims that such forgetfulness is a very condition of action. While it may well be true that the law is not best read in its own terms, "that does not mean that the law is best not *practiced* in its own terms, for it is only by deploying its own terms confidently and without metacritical reservation that it can be practiced at all" (177).

Anticipating the objections of critics, Fish is quick to point out that in describing and defending the law's rhetoricity he is neither defending nor challenging any specific outcome of any particular case; he's simply explaining how the law works.[4] He refuses to engage in the typical "theoretical" effort to connect a description of the law's operations to an evaluation of the correctness of certain decisions. Says Fish,

> In my view, the legal process is always the same, an open, though bounded, forum where forensic battles are contingently and temporarily won; therefore, preferred outcomes are to be achieved not by changing the game but by playing it more effectively (and what is and is not "more effective" is itself something that cannot be known in advance). (178)

That is, the outcomes of legal cases are argued and won rhetorically; they are not won by applying some principle or theory external to the contingencies of the case, and Fish's description of the law's rhetoricity should not be seen as yet another effort to connect a description of how the law works to any outcome. If he were to claim to be able to make such a connection, he will have fallen into the same epistemological trap that he accuses others of falling into: claiming to provide a theoretical perspective from which practice can be guided or reformed. Put differently, his analysis of law's rhetoricity simply will have no consequences.

Rhetoric and the Justification of Belief

> There is no opposition between knowledge by reason and knowledge by faith. . . .
> —Stanley Fish

> What you believe is what you see is what you know is what you do is what you are.
> —Stanley Fish (and John Milton)

For nearly a half a century, scholars from practically every intellectual discipline have asserted a strong connection between rhetoric and epistemology. From Clifford Geertz to Thomas Kuhn, from Richard Rorty to the feminist standpoint theorists, scholar after scholar, despite their disagreements with each other on a multitude of issues, has affirmed the centrality of rhetoric in the making of knowledge. No one has been as consistent and undaunted in this endeavor as Stanley Fish. One factor that sets Fish apart from so many other writers, however, is his belief that our convictions are what have the strongest hold on us and that we then seek to justify those convictions rhetorically, not the other way around. As he comments in "Consequences," beliefs are a "prerequisite for being conscious"; they are "not what you think *about* but what you think *with*, and it is within the space provided by their articulations that mental activity—including the activity of theorizing—goes on. . . . [B]eliefs have *you*, in the sense that there can be no distance between them and the acts they enable" (326). People don't arrive at a position or belief because they have been persuaded by the logic or "reasonableness" of someone's argument; they arrive at a position or belief because it fits into the structure of beliefs already in play. They then seek the available means of persuasion to justify that belief, both to themselves and to others. Rhetoric, then, is not simply a rational, cognitive, mechanical operation as so many other scholars posit. This strong connection between rhetoric and belief is what distinguishes Fish's work.

Although Fish makes this point in a multitude of places throughout his *oeuvre,* one particularly cogent statement is "Faith Before Reason," a short essay exploring the relationship between religious faith and rational inquiry. This essay is a response to Father Richard Neuhaus, editor of *First Things: A Monthly Journal of Religion and Public Life.* Neuhaus had written a reply to Fish's "Why We Can't All Just Get Along," which had appeared earlier in that journal.[5] Fish argues that faith and reason are not in opposition; they are, in fact, mutually interdependent. Put succinctly, the difference between a believer and a nonbeliever (or any two individuals who hold differing beliefs) is not that one reasons and the other doesn't, or that one is rational and the other isn't; rather, each reasons from a central premise that the other denies. While a believer and a nonbeliever may well employ the same rules of evidence and the same kind of rational deliberation, they eventually will disagree about whether something does or does not constitute evidence, and such a disagreement cannot be settled by an appeal to the rules of reason because those rules "unfold in relation to a proposition they do not generate." In the context of a debate between a believer and a nonbeliever, the proposition "God exists or does not exist" is an article of faith, and despite the meticulousness of their adherence to strict rules of logical reasoning, both parties will necessarily end up in "completely different places" precisely because "it is from different (substantive) places that they began" (263). Each begins not from a logical argument but from a heartfelt conviction, and all logical reasoning, justification, and argumentation flows from that conviction.

Because a believer and a nonbeliever each begins from a different premise, a premise the other disavows, each will fashion any evidence that emerges into a shape that is dictated by the structure of his or her belief system. The belief system in play determines how all evidence will be read (interpreted) and how an individual will then be able to turn around and justify a belief and corresponding evidence rhetorically. In other words, we each begin from a position, a conviction, and that conviction and the structure of beliefs to which it is attached will cause us to interpret evidence in such a way as to buttress that conviction and belief system and to repulse challenges to them. We cannot rise above or step outside of our belief system in order to assess evidence or arguments. The central beliefs of a belief system—Christianity, for example— cannot be falsified or even challenged by "evidence" that a believer does not acknowledge (because of that very structure of beliefs) qualifies as evidence: "For one party, falsification follows from the absence of any rational account of how the purported phenomena (walking on water, feeding five thousand with five loaves and two fishes, rising from the dead) could have occurred; for the other the absence of a rational explanation is just the point, one that, far from challenging the faith, confirms it" (268). One's structure of beliefs is likely to be much deeper and much more compelling than any rationalizing that transpires detached from that structure.

An atheist, for example, might point to the Holocaust as clear evidence that God does not exist. If God is merciful and watches over all the world's creatures, then God never would have allowed such unimaginable atrocities to occur. Since these unimaginable atrocities did occur, then surely God cannot exist. The atheist's structure of beliefs causes him or her to receive the information about the Holocaust as confirmation of his or her belief system, and then this information becomes rhetorical support for an argument demonstrating the nonexistence of God. Confronted with information about the Holocaust, a believer might simply contend that such atrocities say more about humanity than about God and may thus dismiss such "evidence" as irrelevant to a discussion about the existence of God—as not evidence at all. Or the believer may well wrestle with the apparent contradiction between unimaginable atrocities and a merciful God, and if that believer could not simply dismiss the information as irrelevant or could not incorporate the information into his or her belief system, that individual would be in a "crisis of faith." But, says Fish, whatever that believer "did with the doubt, it will have been a doubt *for him* by virtue of what he believed and not because a challenge to his belief has come from someplace outside it" (268). Evidence (information, arguments) external to an individual's belief system is not powerful enough in and of itself to shake a person's faith or convictions; only doubt already lodged within the person's belief system would be sufficiently compelling to have such an effect.

In response to such arguments, Neuhaus contends that if an archeological expedition were to establish beyond a reasonable doubt that the remains of a certain body was that of Jesus Christ, then the truth claims of Christianity would be in grave doubt. But Fish replies that this depends on how one construes "reasonable doubt":

> If he means the kind of doubt an empirically minded nonbeliever might have, then the doubt is a foregone conclusion since it is implicit in the way he (already) thinks. "A virgin birth? A God incarnate? Give me a break!" But if Neuhaus means a reasonable doubt a Christian might have, then it would have to be a doubt raised by tensions internal to Christian belief, and not by tensions *between* Christian belief and some other belief system. (268)

The believer and the nonbeliever each adjusts incoming evidence to his or her belief system, shaping the information to support that structure of beliefs and dismissing as irrelevant anything that contradicts it. It would take much more than carbon dating to shake or topple a faith that is not founded on such kinds of evidence in the first place because carbon dating qualifies as evidence only in the context of assumptions that the believer does not share and, in fact, considers to be unequivocally wrong. Someone who believes a view to be correct simply cannot see what is seen by those who deny its very founding premises, and vice versa.

One might argue (as Neuhaus does) that people often encounter propositions that they can fully understand but that they nonetheless believe to be untrue. There is a substantial difference, however, between comprehending the literal meaning of a proposition and experiencing the truth of that utterance in a deeply heartfelt way. It is one matter to understand the semantics and syntax of an utterance; it is entirely another matter to inhabit the position that the utterance announces. These are two different senses of what it means to "understand." You might announce that you understand a statement and that it is untrue, but "understand" in this sense means that from your perspective the assertion has the form of a truth statement but no valid content: you understand it to be nothing, and consequently you understand it only in the most superficial sense—that is, you in effect do not understand it at all. Thus, in response to Neuhaus' declaration that a Christian can "understand" what an atheist is saying, Fish replies, "Sure he can: he will understand the atheist as saying error, that which is not" (270). The Christian may well comprehend the syntax and semantics of the atheist's declaration that God is a fiction, but because the believer begins from a first premise that is totally antithetical to the atheist's first premise, the Christian is unable to inhabit the position that the utterance announces—the atheist's statement, then, is truly incomprehensible to the believer, except in the most superficial way.

For Fish, then, people arrive at a position or belief because it fits into the structure of beliefs already in play, not because they have been swayed by the "reasonableness" of someone's argument; they then pursue the available means of support to justify that belief rhetorically, both to themselves and to others. People "understand" or are "persuaded" by a position or belief because it fits into a preexisting belief structure. This description of the relationship between faith and reason, rhetoric and epistemology is in sharp contrast to the prevailing liberal-humanist perspective that emerges from the tradition of Enlightenment rationality—a tradition that regards the mind as a kind of "calculating and assessing machine that is open to all thoughts and closed to none." In this rationalist conception, belief and knowledge are discrete and independent, and the mind is never closed, always open; in fact, committing to a value or idea in a fixed way is a sure sign of "cognitive and moral infirmity"—what is often labeled "closed mindedness" or "blind belief" ("Why" 247). Fish contends, however, that the mind must begin with a first premise, a fixed commitment to a value or idea, and this premise both enables thought about the subject at hand and is unavailable to thought precisely because it is thought's enabling condition: "One's consciousness must be grounded in an originary act of faith [about anything, not just religious issues]—a stipulation of basic value—from which determinations of right and wrong, relevant and irrelevant, real and unreal, will then follow" (247). For the liberal rationalist, the mind operates independent of any particular belief, coolly and rationally assessing contending beliefs to determine which make sense; for Fish, beliefs are the "content of a rationality that cannot scrutinize them because it rests on them," in the sense that rationality arises from beliefs and not the other way around (247). Consequently, Fish would exchange the liberal motto "Seeing is believing" for the seemingly counterintuitive "Believing is seeing," signifying that it is our beliefs that enable us to see in certain ways and not others. Furthermore, because what we see constitutes the boundary or limits of our knowledge, what we believe is coextensive with what we know (believing is knowing). And further, since we typically base our actions on what we know, then believing is acting; and since it is our actions that constitute who we are, in many ways we are what we believe. Put epigrammatically, "What you believe is what you see is what you know is what you do is what you are"—or, we are what we believe (247).

In a very real way, then, liberal open mindedness is impossible, in that we are never truly open to beliefs that flow from premises hostile to the premises and beliefs we begin with. We call a belief or position (and the person who utters it) "reasonable" when it corresponds to our own beliefs and positions. Because what we consider to be reasonable is based on a submerged core belief that itself determines what reasonableness is, we cannot subject that submerged core belief to a test of reasonableness; that would be tantamount to rising out of our own ideological perspective in order to examine that perspective from outside of itself—which, of course, is impossible. It is the ideological perspective that constitutes us and our notion of reasonableness in the first place. There is nothing outside of our structure of beliefs, then, that we can appeal to in order to validate or adjust our beliefs, no external or neutral arbiter against which to evaluate those beliefs. In fact, this is the thesis of Fish's "Beliefs about Belief." In that essay, he argues that because there is nothing undergirding our beliefs, "nothing to which our beliefs might be referred for either confirmation or correction," there is "nothing interesting to say about belief in general" (279). That is, belief is a particular, not a general; it arises out of a particular person's belief system under certain conditions and in specific contexts. There is no general way to characterize it or its operations since it is radically contingent.

Fish has consistently stated that an individual's belief about belief has no relationship to any particular belief the person might hold, unless the question being considered happens to be the nature of belief: "The thesis, baldly put, is that anything one believes about a particular matter is logically independent of the account one might give (and how many of us after all could give such an account) of how beliefs emerge or of what underlies them or of what confirms them or calls them into question" (280). A meta-level (theoretical) discussion of how beliefs are formed is disconnected from and of no consequence to a person's specific beliefs. One person may believe that his or her beliefs are firmly grounded in some solid foundation—God, truth, reason—and another may believe that beliefs are never supported by general principles detached from specific contexts and that if only everybody would arrive at this realization people would stop using their beliefs as the justification for social conflict, including war; however, both views somehow presume that a belief about belief can in some way have some general significance or repercussion. Neither of these two individuals' differing conceptions of the workings of belief will affect their respective beliefs; these individuals will not abandon their beliefs or alter them or exchange them or believe in them less or more firmly: "That is because there is no *relationship* between us and our beliefs; rather, there is an identity. The operations of my consciousness and the shape of my beliefs are not two entities somehow 'relating' to one another but one entity called by different names" (280). Beliefs are constitutive of consciousness and thus cannot exist independent of consciousness. This is yet another way to say that we are what we believe.

To say that beliefs are constitutive of consciousness is not to say that beliefs are groundless or have no support; rather, beliefs are supported by other beliefs in an intricate structure of beliefs, "a lattice or a web whose component parts are mutually constitutive." A person who is asked to justify a particular belief or position will immediately appeal to "the interlocking structure of understandings within which the particular belief in question seems obvious" (280, 281). Asked to support a belief about evolution, an individual would draw on theories of scientific evidence, a vocabulary of "genes" and "mutations," and a theory about the origins of life. Every fact and assumption proffered to bolster the position may in turn require support, in which case the individual would "point to those components of the picture not presently under the pressure of a demand for justification." While this process may well be circular, it is circular in the same way that the operation of a dictionary is circular: "one meaning explains another which explains another, which, somewhere down the line, is explained by the meaning with which you began" (281). We justify a belief, then, by turning to the structure of beliefs from which the belief derives its intelligibility and within which it is coherent, and we then seek to express that intelligibility and coherence rhetorically, establishing a case for the belief.

One might object to this description of a structure of beliefs and the rhetorical justification of belief by claiming that it does not account for how beliefs change. That is, if the structure of beliefs is composed of a latticework of mutually supportive beliefs and if the justification of belief is internal to that structure, what force or incentive could impel change? Fish replies that belief itself is the cause of a change in belief, and this will only seem paradoxical if beliefs are assumed to be discrete and independent entities; beliefs, however, are "components of a structure and exist in relationships of dependence and scope to one another, and among the beliefs internal to any structure will be a belief as to what might be a reason for its own revision" (281). Every individual will have his or her own threshold as to what might cause a belief to change, and there is no way to predict in advance what that threshold might be. As an example, Fish cites the case of a white supremacist who abandoned his former colleagues, renounced his previously heartfelt racist ideology, and worked to publicize the dangers of the white supremacist movement. This neo-Nazi, whose daughter had a cleft palate, repudiated his previous worldview after his group's leader publicly denounced the physically disabled. This narrative of instant conversion illustrates that it is not possible to generalize a model of change from specific instances of change; each instance is so unique and context dependent that no useful general account of change could be extrapolated from one instance. What's more, there was no way to predict in advance that the neo-Nazi whose daughter had a cleft palate would renounce his faith; he might have responded by professing renewed allegiance to his group on the grounds that "the cause" was greater than any single individual, including his daughter. Explanations of a change in belief will always be constructed ex post facto, and no retrospective account of a change in belief will be useful in predicting what that person is likely to do in the future. Fish writes,

> Any authority, no matter how longstanding its hold on your imagination, can be dislodged in an instant, although that instant cannot be willed, cannot be planned for, and need not ever occur. But if it does, it will not be because an independent reality has presented itself in such a way that a structure of belief must simply bow to it but because embedded in that structure will be something—an allegiance, a fear, a hope—that is strongly affirmed in a crisis of decision or choice. The moment of its affirmation will be the moment at which the web of belief might undergo a basic alteration—you could leave the cult you have lived for or abandon the argument that has made your career—but the mechanics of that alteration will be entirely internal. (283)

The insularity of a structure of beliefs does not preclude the ability to change a belief; it is the very mechanism that enables the ability to change a belief.

In many ways, we have little control over our beliefs. No one shops for a belief and then consciously chooses one from an array of competing beliefs; rather, the act of believing is involuntary, more a matter of reflex than cogitation. Acquiring a belief is more akin to catching a cold than to selecting a new shirt.[6] Nor can we simply refrain from believing our beliefs through an act of will. Belief operates at a much deeper, subterranean level. This is why Fish says that we don't "have" beliefs; beliefs "have" us. To say that we don't have beliefs but that beliefs have us is not to suggest that beliefs or the actions that proceed from them are "irrational"; rather, it is to affirm that rationality—which includes the rhetorical processes of collecting evidence, providing examples and support, refuting opposing arguments, correcting errors, and so on— takes place "in the light of our beliefs." That is, belief precedes rationality. Or, put another way, rationality operates within a "context of convictions and commitments it neither chooses nor approves" (284).

If beliefs are constitutive of consciousness, if we are what we believe, then we have no access to how those beliefs operate; they are not accessible to the conscious mind, since access would assume that we could rise above them. The fact that we cannot rise above them is precisely why we can't, through an act of will, choose or reject or analyze them. Most importantly, it is only within our belief system that "deliberation occurs and evidence becomes perspicuous and reasons persuasive" (284). That is, rhetoric transpires within—in fact is enabled by and in turn helps justify—a belief system. Far from the simple mechanical process of marshaling the available means of support, rhetoric arises from and is part of the complex workings of an intricate web of beliefs altogether unavailable to consciousness. Rhetoric, then, is truly fundamental to how humans operate in the world. This is why Fish and others like him are moving rhetoric from "the disreputable periphery to the necessary center," for if the "highest truth" for any given person is what that person believes it to be,[7] then the skill that justifies belief and "therefore establishes what, in a particular time and a particular place, is true, is the skill essential to the building and maintaining of a civilized society. In the absence of a revealed truth, rhetoric is that skill" ("Rhetoric" 480).

Chapter 4

Fish Tales: A Conversation with "The Contemporary Sophist"

Perhaps one reason why Stanley Fish influences so many of us in rhetoric and composition is that he has always insisted that rhetoric is *central*, that it's the "necessary center," that "substantial realities are products of rhetorical, persuasive, political efforts." As Fish says in the interview that follows, once you "begin with a sense of the constructed nature of human reality," then rhetoric is "reconceived as the medium in which certainties become established." It's no wonder, then, that Fish feels comfortable being called a social constructionist. Nor is it surprising that he finds "perfectly appropriate" Roger Kimball's label for him: "the contemporary sophist." In fact, Fish sees an affinity between sophism and the anti-foundationalist project he has so long championed. He credits his work with Milton, his first love and still a driving passion in his intellectual life, as the genesis of his struggle against essentialist, foundationalist philosophies: as an antinomian Christian and an "absolutely severe anti-formalist," Milton was "rather far down the anti-foundationalist road."

Another reason for Fish's influence in rhetoric and composition is his continued interest in and support of composition. He remains conversant with the discipline's intellectual developments, and he even goes so far as to say that much of his thinking about theory and anti-foundationalism was formed in the early 1960s when he taught composition classes using Walker Gibson's *The Limits of Language*: "The essays in that book were perhaps the most powerful influence on me." As always, Fish is outspoken about intellectual trends he disapproves of, and certain developments in composition are no exception. He is skeptical of attempts to "teach people that situational experience is in fact always primary" because he believes this "theoretical" lesson will not produce any generalizable result. On the other hand, he favors training in which composition students are placed in realistic scenarios and are asked to write to the scenario. The difference, in Fish's view, is that the first is an attempt to teach students a "theoretical" perspective in the hopes that they can then apply that perspective to particular situations—something that just cannot happen, according to Fish. The second, however, is experience or practice in specific contexts—for Fish the only "real" knowledge. He repeats, "The practice of training students to be able to adjust their verbal performances to different registers of social life requires no theoretical assumptions whatsoever."

Clearly, this position is consistent with his larger campaign over the years "against theory." Says Fish, "I'm a localist. . . . I believe in rules of thumb." That is, he believes intensely in here-and-now situationality; to believe otherwise would be to subscribe to "the fetishization of the unified self and a whole lot of other things that as 'postmodernists' we are supposedly abandoning." Thus, he discounts attempts to cultivate critical self-consciousness, another type of *theoretical* capacity: "Insofar as critical self-consciousness is a possible human achievement, it requires no special ability and cannot be cultivated as an independent value apart from particular situations."

Fish also comments on other issues in composition scholarship. Retreating somewhat from his earlier criticism of Kenneth Bruffee, Fish acknowledges that collaborative learning *can* be productive. But we must not assume, he cautions, that somehow it is inherently superior to other modes of instruction; it is simply "different," each pedagogical strategy having its own "gains and losses." And while he refuses to embrace radical pedagogy, he sees it as "*a* wave of the future." He himself prefers a more traditional arrangement: perceiving the classroom as "a performance occasion," he enjoys "orchestrating the class," noting that no one would ever mistake one of his classes for "a participatory democracy." He quips that he would never adopt liberatory techniques for two very good reasons: "too much egocentrism, too much of a long career as a professional theatrical academic."

In addition, Fish expresses genuine respect for feminism and the influence it has exerted on the intellectual life of society because, for Fish, it has passed the key test that indicates the "true power of a form of inquiry": when "the assumptions encoded in the vocabulary of a form of thought become inescapable in the larger society." He believes that the questions raised by feminism "have energized more thought and social action than any other 'ism' in the past twenty or thirty years." Nevertheless, he does not support feminists "who rely in their arguments on a distinction between male and female epistemologies." Such feminists, he feels, fall prey to the same epistemological difficulties as those who champion critical self-consciousness: a belief that "you can in some way step back from, rise above, get to the side of your beliefs and convictions so that they will have less of a hold on you."

Fish addresses numerous other issues, such as the nature of "intentional structures" and "forceful interpretive acts," the bankruptcy of the liberal intellectual agenda, and the obligation of academics to engage in what Noam Chomsky has called "more socially useful activities." He is particularly concerned about how the larger societal turn toward conservatism is affecting higher education, and he predicts a period of curtailment and purges so long as the well-financed neo-conservative political agenda continues to be "backed by huge amounts of right-wing foundation money." The solution is for academics to speak out to audiences beyond the academy, to help explain intellectual developments to the general public in order to counter narrow conservative perspectives: "I think we *must* talk back."

It may seem something of a paradox that Stanley Fish, who argues so vociferously *against* theory, is becoming more influential in composition studies precisely at a time when the field, or at least part of it, is busily engaged in *theory building*. Yet while the role of theory in rhetoric and composition may still be uncertain, it *is* clear that Fish is in many ways an ally. Especially as more compositionists explore social construction and the role of rhetoric in epistemology, Fish's work becomes increasingly relevant. Responding to criticism from both the intellectual right and left, Fish insists that harkening to him will not "lead to the decay of civilization," nor will it "lead to the canonization of the status quo." Harkening to Fish, however, *may* well lead to productive avenues of inquiry for many of us in composition.

Olson: In *Doing What Comes Naturally*, you speak of this as the age of rhetoric and the "world of *homo rhetoricus*." You yourself are frequently called a rhetorician *par excellence*. But do you consider yourself a writer?

Fish: I do in some ways. Last night at the Milton Society of America banquet I spoke of the influence on me of C.S. Lewis. I think of C.S. Lewis and J.L. Austin as the two stylists I've tried to imitate in a variety of ways, and so I'm very self-conscious about the way I craft sentences. I always feel that once I get a particular sentence right I can go on to the next, and I don't go on to the next until I think it's right. In the sense that this is not just superficially but centrally a concern, I consider myself a writer. In other senses—for example, whether I expect people to be studying my works long after my demise—the answer is that I do *not* consider myself a writer. But the craft I think of myself as practicing is the craft of writing, and my obsession there is a very old-fashioned one, a canonical one, a traditional one—and that is clarity.

Olson: What you describe is exactly how Clifford Geertz described *his* writing process recently in *JAC*. Would you tell us more about your writing process? Do you revise frequently? Use a computer?

Fish: I do not use a computer and I do not revise. I now use one of those small electronic typewriters that you can move around and take on so-called vacations. That's about as far as I've advanced in the age of mechanical reproduction. Since my writing practices are as I just described, I don't tend to revise. I go back occasionally and reposition an adverb, and I often go through my manuscripts and cross out what I know to be some of my tics. For example, I use the phrase *of course* too much, I often double nouns and verbs for no particular reason, and I have other little favorite mannerisms that I've learned to recognize and eliminate. But very rarely do I ever restructure an essay or even a paragraph.

Olson: That's surprising considering your polished style. I should have thought you spent countless hours revising.

Fish: Well, I write slowly. My pace is two pages a day when I'm writing well, when I have a sense of where the particular essay is or should be going. That's often when I sit for six to eight hours and am continually engaged in the process of thinking through the essay. Also, I do this often (not always, but often) while watching television. This is a very old habit. Actually, this is a talent (if it is a talent) that more people of the younger generation have today than people of my generation. But I've always been able to do it. To this day when I reread something I've written I can remember what television program I was watching when

I wrote it. I remember once when I was in Madrid and went to the bullfights, I wrote a passage about Book Six of *Paradise Lost*; every time I look at it I remember that I was watching the bullfights when I wrote it.

Olson: As an English department chair, what are your thoughts about the future of rhetoric and composition as a discipline? What role will it (or should it) play in the modern English department?

Fish: I don't know because I don't know whether there will be something called "the modern English department" in the next twenty years. I had thought, in fact, that there would be a more accelerated transformation of the traditional English department than there has yet been. My prediction ten years ago had been that by the year 2000 the English department in which we were all educated would be a thing of the past, a museum piece, represented certainly in some places but supplanted in most others by departments of literature, departments of cultural studies, departments of humanistic interrogation, or departments of literacy. That hasn't happened in the rapid way I thought it would; there are *some* places, like the Syracuse University, and earlier modes of experimentation, like the University of California at San Diego, Rensselaer Polytech, and others, but not as many as I thought there would be. If the change, when it comes, goes in the same direction that Syracuse has pioneered, then it might be just as accurate to call the department "the department of rhetoric," with a new understanding of the old scope of the subject and province of rhetoric. That's a possibility, but I'm less confident now than I was ten years ago about such predictions. For one thing, the economic difficulties we've been experiencing lately have had a great effect on the academy. Two years ago the job market looked extraordinarily promising, and certain kinds of pressures that departments had always felt seemed to be lessening. There would therefore have been an atmosphere in which experimentation and transformation might have been more possible. But now that we have had a return of a sense of constricted economy and constricted possibilities and everybody is talking retrenchment (an awful word, but one that you hear more and more), it may be that the current departmental sense of the university structure may continue because the protection of interests that are now in place becomes a strong motive once a threat to the entire structure is perceived. And certainly many people are now perceiving a threat to the entire structure.

Olson: So for progress, we need prosperity.

Fish: Absolutely, and especially in the humanities. Two or five or ten years ago, none of us would have predicted the current *political* assault on humanities education and the attempt to—and this is perhaps the least plausible scapegoating effort in the history of scapegoating, which is a very long history—blame all the country's ills on what is being done in a few classrooms by teachers of English and French. It is truly incredible that this story of why the moral fiber of the United States has been weakened has found such acceptance, but it has and now these consequences are ones we have to deal with in some way.

Olson: During a talk at the University of South Florida, you repeated on several occasions that you are a "very traditional" teacher who uses "very traditional methods." In *JAC*, Derrida characterized his own teaching in much the same way. Yet in English studies now, especially in rhetoric and composition, there's a movement toward "liberatory learning," radicalizing the classroom and breaking down its traditional power structures by attempting to disperse authority among all participants. What are your thoughts about radical pedagogy in general and its altering of the teacher-student hierarchy specifically?

Fish: Well, my thoughts about radical pedagogy are complicated by the fact that my wife, Jane Tompkins, is a radical pedagogue and moves more and more in that direction; she writes essays and gives talks that command what I would almost call a cult following. I've seen some of these performances. *That* at least tells me that there's something out there to which she and others are appealing. I have *some* sense—which one might call an anthropological sense—of what that something is. But I'm simply too deeply embedded in and too much a product of my own education and practices to make or even to want to make that turn. I would first have to feel some dissatisfaction with my current mode of teaching or with the experiences of my classroom, and I don't feel that. For me the classroom is still what she has formally renounced: a performance occasion. And I enjoy the performances; I enjoy orchestrating the class in ways that involve students in the performances, but no one is under any illusion that this is a participatory (or any other kind) of democracy in a class of mine. However, having said this I should hasten to add that my own disinclination to turn in that direction does not lead me to label that direction as evil, wayward, irresponsible, unsound, or any of the usual adjectives that follow. It seems to me quite clear that this is, if not *the* wave of the future, *a* wave of the future. In fact, I listened to some of the interviews for our assistant director of composition position yesterday, and every one of the interviewees I talked to identified himself or herself as a person interested in just this new kind of liberatory, new age, holistic, collaborative teaching. So I think it is the wave of the future, and I would certainly welcome those who are dedicated. But I'm sure that I would never do it myself—too much egocentrism, too much of a long career as a professional theatrical academic.

Olson: You disagree with Patricia Bizzell and those who encourage us to teach students the "discourse conventions" of their disciplines, arguing that "being told that you are in a situation will help you neither to dwell in it more perfectly nor to *write* within it more successfully." Surely, though, you don't really advise compositionists *not* to teach students that there are numerous discourse communities, each with characteristic discourse conventions? Wouldn't we be remiss to ignore such considerations in our pedagogies?

Fish: Of course, I quite agree. My objection in that essay—an objection I make in other essays in slightly different terms—is to the assumption that if we teach people that situational experience is in fact always primary and that one never reasons from a set of portable and invariant theses or propositions to specific situations (that is, one is always within a situation in relation to which some propositions seem relevant and others seem out in left field), if you just teach that as a theoretical lesson and walk away from the class and expect something to happen, the only thing that will happen is that the next time you ask that particular question, you'll get that particular answer. However, I do believe in training of a kind familiar to students of classical and medieval rhetoric—training, let's say, of the Senecan kind, in which one is placed by one's instructor in a situation: you are attempting to cross a river; there is only one ferry; you have to persuade the ferryman to do this or that, and he is disinclined to do so for a number of given reasons—what do you then do? That kind of training, transposed into a modern mode, is essential. I don't think it need be accompanied by any epistemological rap. What I was objecting to in Pat's essay—and I was to some extent being captious because in general I am an admirer of her work—was the suggestion that the theoretical perspective on situationality itself could do work if transmitted to a group of students. I think that one could teach that way, and many have—that is, they've taught situational performance and the pressures and obligations that go with being in situations—without ever having been within a thousand miles of a theoretical thought.

Olson: But isn't this inconsistent with everything you say about rhetoric in the larger sense, that to be a good rhetorician is to know situatedness?

Fish: It depends on what you mean by "to know situatedness." There's one sense in which to know situatedness is to be on one side of a debate about the origins of knowledge, to be on the side that locates knowledge or finds the location of knowledge in the temporal structure of particular situations. That's to know situatedness in the sense that one might call either theoretical or philosophical. Now to know situatedness in the sense of being able to code switch, to operate successfully in different registers, is something else, and you don't even have to use the vocabulary that accompanies most theoretical discussions of these points. I was a teacher of composition long ago (relatively—thirty years ago) before any of us in the world of literary studies knew the word *theory* (Ah, for those days! Bliss was it in those times to be alive!), and many people taught what we would now call situational performance; and there were many routes to that teaching. So again, my point always is that the practice of training students to be able to adjust their verbal performances to different registers of social life requires no theoretical assumptions whatsoever. They are required neither of the instructor, and certainly not of the student.

Olson: Kenneth Bruffee draws heavily on you and Richard Rorty to formulate his version of collaborative learning theory. Rorty has already distanced himself from Bruffee's project, and you criticize it because it "becomes a new and fashionable version of democratic liberalism, a political vision that has at its center the goal of disinterestedly viewing contending partisan perspectives which are then either reconciled or subsumed in some higher or more general synthesis, in a larger and larger *consensus*." Given one of the major (and typical) alternatives—a teacher-dominated classroom and an information-transfer model of education—and given the fact that much of your own life's work has been devoted to illustrating how interpretive communities work, wouldn't you agree that Bruffee's collaborative learning is productive despite his own naive liberalism?

Fish: Yes, it could be. I think that's an excellent point. I don't know whether it is, but there's nothing to prevent it from being productive. That is, collaborative learning is a mode of knowledge production *different* from other modes of knowledge production. In my view, differences are always real; however, differences should never be ranked on a scale of more or less real. So to refine what might be a point of contest between Bruffee and me, I would agree with him that if we move into a mode of collaborative learning, *different* things will happen, things which probably would not have been available under other modes. Also, *some* possibilities will be lost. I tend to think of pedagogical strategies as strategies each of which has its gains and losses. I also believe that there are times in the history of a culture or a discipline when it's time to switch strategies, not because a teleology pulls us in the direction of this or that one, but because the one in which we've been operating has at the moment taken us about as far as we can go and so perhaps we ought to try something else—which, as you will have recognized, has a kind of Rortian ring to it.

Olson: Yes, it does. In fact, let me ask you a related question. Your essay "Change" is a detailed discussion of how interpretive communities change their beliefs and assumptions, and in making the argument that "no theory can compel change" you say that we should think of the community not as an "object" of change but as "an engine of change." Although you don't use Rorty's vocabulary of "normal" and "abnormal discourse," like Rorty you seem to be arguing against the notion that substantive disciplinary or intellectual change transpires as a result of persuasive abnormal discourse. What are your thoughts on the role of abnormal discourse as a catalyst of change?

Fish: I think that abnormal discourse *can* be a catalyst of change, and that's because I think that *anything* can be a catalyst of change. This goes back to a series of points I've been making "against theory" for a number of years now. One of my arguments is that strong-theory proponents attribute to theory a unique capacity for producing change and often believe (and this is perhaps a parody) that if we can only get our epistemology straight, or get straight our account of the subject, then important political and material things will follow. It's that sense of the kind of change that will follow from a new theoretical argument that I reject. However, theory—or as I sometimes say tendentiously in these essays, "theory talk"—can like anything else be the catalyst of change, but it's a contingent and historical matter; it depends on the history of the particular community, the kinds of talk or vocabularies that have prestige or cachet or are likely to trump other kinds of talk. And if in a certain community the sense of what is at stake is highly intermixed with a history of theoretical discourse, then in *that* community at *that* time a change in practices may be produced by a change in theory.

Of course, "abnormal" discourse comes in a variety of forms. For example, if one takes the term "discourse" in its larger senses, one can think that a recession is an abnormal form of discourse, that suddenly one's ordinary ways of conceiving of one's situation are complicated by facts that a year or two ago would have seemed to belong in another realm. Abnormal discourse can always erupt into the routine structures of an interpretive community, but there's no way to predict in advance which ones will in fact erupt and with what effects.

Olson: Well, Rorty claimed in *JAC* that abnormal discourse is "a gift of God," while Geertz prefers a less grandiose notion he calls "nonstandard discourse." For Rorty this happens rarely; for Geertz it occurs all the time. Obviously, these are two different conceptions of abnormal discourse. Does either one seem more useful than the other?

Fish: Not really. I'm not sure whether Rorty and Geertz are making this assumption, but it could be that one or both of them is assuming that abnormal discourse is itself a stable category, and it seems to me that what is or is not abnormal in relation to a discourse history will itself be contingent. For example, in some literary communities that I know about and that I'm a participant in, it now becomes "abnormal" to begin a class by saying, "Today we will explicate Donne's 'The Good-Morrow.'" *That* would be, at least in some classrooms at Duke, a *dazzling* move—not, I hasten to add, in *mine*, because that's a practice I've never ceased to engage in.

Olson: Both you and Rorty have been cited as two of the principal intellectual sources of social construction; however, when I asked Rorty in an earlier interview if he considered himself a social constructionist he seemed baffled by the appellation. Despite your understandable resistance to limiting categories, and given your continual insistence that everything is rhetorical and situated, would you consider *yourself* a social constructionist?

Fish: In a certain sense I would say, "Sure." If I were to be asked a series of questions relevant to a tradition of inquiry in which several accounts of the origin of knowledge or facticity were given, I would come out on the side that could reasonably be labeled "social constructionism." I myself have not made elaborate arguments for a social constructionist view—though I've used such arguments at points in my writing—but I have no problem being identified as someone who would support that view.

Olson: In the essay "Rhetoric" you examine the history of anti-rhetorical thought and the unchanging "status of rhetoric in relation to a foundational vision of truth and meaning." You state, "Whether the center of that vision is a personalized deity or an abstract geometric reason, rhetoric is the force that pulls us away from the center and into its own world of ever-shifting shapes and shimmering surfaces." You contrast this mainstream tradition with a counter tradition, represented in classical times by the sophists and today by the anti-foundationalists, whom you credit with helping to move "rhetoric from the disreputable periphery to the necessary center." First, in establishing rhetoric as a kind of master category, don't you run the risk of what Derrida has warned of in *JAC* and elsewhere: rhetoricism, "thinking that everything depends on rhetoric"?

Fish: What is his point? What's the risk?

Olson: He claims that rhetoricism leads us down an essentialist path. His definition is literally that rhetoricism is "thinking that everything depends on rhetoric." It seems to me very different from what *you* say.

Fish: I'm surprised to hear that answer from Derrida because it seems to buy back into a view of the rhetorical that would oppose it to something more substantial, whereas in my view substantial realities are products of rhetorical, persuasive, political efforts. When discussing these matters with committed foundationalists, of whom there are still huge numbers, one always is aware that for them the notion of rhetoric only makes sense as a category of inferiority in relation to something more substantial. For someone who listens with a certain set of ears, the assertion of the primacy of rhetoric can only be heard either as an evil gesture in which "the real" is being overwhelmed, or as a gesture of despair in which either a hedonistic amorality or paralysis must follow. All of these responses to the notion of the persuasiveness of rhetoric are, of course, holding on for dear life to a paradigm in which the rhetorical only enters as the evil shadow of the real. If, on the other hand, you begin with a sense of the constructed nature of human reality (one leaves the ontological question aside if one has half a brain), then the notion of the rhetorical is no longer identified with the ephemeral, the outside, but is reconceived as the medium in which certainties become established, in which formidable traditions emerge, are solidified, and become obstacles (not insurmountable ones, but nevertheless obstacles) to the force of counter-rhetorical movements. So I would give an answer like that to what might seem to be one reading of Derrida's warning, though I am loathe to put *him* anywhere near the camp of those whose thoughts I was describing, since he's a man, as everyone knows, of extraordinary power of intelligence.

Olson: Then do you conceive of the project of the anti-foundationalists as an extension or resurgence of sophism?

Fish: I think that's one helpful way of conceiving of it, and it's helpful in a rhetorical sense. Roger Kimball, in *The New Criterion*, wrote an essay that I think later became part of *Tenured Radicals: How Politics Has Corrupted Our Higher Education.* I don't know what the title of the essay is in *Tenured Radicals*, but in *The New Criterion* the essay on me was entitled "The Contemporary Sophist." He meant that as a derogatory label, but I thought it was perfectly appropriate. To call oneself a sophist is rhetorically effective at the moment because you seem to be confessing to a crime. If you begin by saying, "I am a sophist," and then begin unashamedly to explain why for you this is not a declaration of moral guilt, it's a nice effective move; it catches your audience's attention. So I think that right now there's some mileage (although it's mileage that's attended by danger, too) in identifying the new emphasis on rhetoric with the older tradition of the sophists.

Olson: Recently in *JAC* Clifford Geertz said that Kenneth Burke was one of two thinkers who had the most influence on him intellectually, the other being Wittgenstein. You yourself have referred to Burke's work from time to time. What is your assessment of Burke's contribution to our ways of thinking about language and rhetoric?

Fish: I don't have a strong assessment. I've read Burke only sporadically and only occasionally and have never made a sustained study of his work and therefore could not say that I have been influenced by it directly. I'm sure that I've been influenced by it in all kinds of ways of which I am unaware because of the persons that I've read or talked to who have themselves been strong Burkeans. I can think of two such people that I've talked to and read a great deal: my old friend Richard Lanham at UCLA and Frank Lentricchia, my colleague at Duke, both of whom are committed Burkeans. No doubt lots of things that they have said to me over the years have passed on a heritage of Burke to me, but I've never myself studied him in an intensive way.

Olson: Who *has* had a major influence on you?

Fish: Well, that's difficult to say. Of course, Milton has been a major influence on me. That would be inescapable having spent thirty years studying his work.

Olson: Milton, the anti-foundationalist?

Fish: Yes, in a way. Milton is an antinomian Christian. That is, he's an absolutely severe anti-formalist. Everyone has always known that about Milton. He is continually rejecting the authority of external forms and even the shape of external forms independently of the spirit or intentional orientation of the believer. In his prose tract called *The Christian Doctrine*, which was only discovered many years after his death, Milton begins the second book, which is devoted to daily life, to works in the world, by asking the obvious question, "What is a good work?" He comes up with the answer that a good work is one that is informed by the working of the Holy Spirit in you. That definition, which I've given you imperfectly, does several things. It takes away the possibility of answering the question "What is a good work?" by producing a list of good works, such as founding hospitals or helping old ladies cross the street. It also takes away the possibility of identifying from the outside whether or not the work a person is doing is good or bad, since goodness or badness would be a function of the Holy Spirit's operation, which is internal and invisible. Milton then seals the point by saying a paragraph or so later that in answer to the question "What is a good work?" some people would say the ten commandments, and therefore give a list. Milton then says, "However, I read in the Bible that *faith* is the obligation of the true Christian, not the ten commandments; therefore, if any one of the commandments is contradictory to my inner sense of what is required, then my obedience to the ten commandments becomes an act of sin." Now, if within two or three paragraphs of your discussion of ethics, which is what the second book of *The Christian Doctrine* is, you have dislodged the ten commandments as the repository of ethical obligation, you are rather far down the anti-foundationalist road. And Milton is a strong antinomian, by which I mean he refuses to flinch in the face of the extraordinary existential anxiety produced by antinomianism. So, much of my thinking about a great many things stems from my study of Milton.

Also, I've been strongly influenced as a prose stylist, as I've already mentioned, by C.S. Lewis and J.L. Austin. In fact, I've been very much influenced by J.L. Austin in my thinking about a great many things in addition to my thinking about how to write certain kinds of English sentences. I've also been influenced by Augustine. It's a curious question to answer because many of the people whom I now regularly cite in essays are people that I read *after* most of the views that found my work were already formed. That is, I hadn't read Kuhn before 1979. I'm fond of citing Kuhn, as a great many other people are. I have found support again and again in the pages of Wittgenstein, but I cannot say that it was a study of Wittgenstein that led me to certain questions or answers.

Let me say one more thing. When I was first starting out as a teacher, I gave the same exam in every course, no matter what the subject matter. The exam was very simple: I asked the students to relate two sentences to each other and to the materials of the course. The first sentence was from J. Robert Oppenheimer: "Style is the deference that action pays to uncertainty." I took that to mean that in a world without certain foundations for action you avoid the Scylla of prideful self-assertion, on the one hand, and the Charybdis of paralysis, on the other hand, by stepping out provisionally, with a sense of limitation, with a sense of style. The other quotation, which I matched and asked the students to consider, is from the first verse of Hebrews Eleven: "Now faith is the substance of things hoped for, the evidence of things not seen." I take that to be the classically theological version of Oppenheimer's statement, and so the question of the relationship between style and faith, or between interpretation and action and certainty, has been the obsessive concern of my thinking since the first time I gave this test back in 1962 or 1963. I think there is *nothing* in my work that couldn't be generated from those two assertions and their interactions. They came from a book I used in my composition teaching from the very beginning, and I don't even know how I came to use it. The essays in that book were perhaps the most powerful influence on me. It's a book edited by Walker Gibson, and it's called *The Limits of Language*. It had this essay by Oppenheimer; essays by Whitehead, Conant, and Percy Bridgman, the Nobel Prize winning physicist; Gertrude Stein's essay on punctuation (which is fantastic); and several others that I used in my classes and that informed my early questionings and giving of answers. That book was an extraordinarily powerful influence. Of course, the quotation from Hebrews Eleven came in from my Milton work.

Olson: You just mentioned finding support in the pages of Wittgenstein. In "Accounting for the Changing Certainties of Interpretive Communities," Reed Way Dasenbrock suggests that your debt to Wittgenstein is far greater than you have yet acknowledged. Do you think Wittgenstein was a major influence on your work?

Fish: No I don't, because I don't know him well enough. Reed was a student of mine. I have a bunch of students out in the world who make what I hope is a very good living writing essays that point out my limitations and flaws, and he's one of them. He no doubt knows Wittgenstein much better than I do and has learned a great deal from him; he therefore probably assumes that I *must* have been influenced by him. Now it *is* true that back in about 1977 or 1978 I was for a semester in a reading group with two or three philosophers from Johns Hopkins: David Sachs, George Wilson, and my friend the art historian,

Michael Fried. We read Wittgenstein and talked about him for a period of months. Somewhat earlier—and here's another influence that I'd forgotten to acknowledge but should have acknowledged—there's probably a larger influence from Heidegger as transmitted to me in a series of courses I attended given by Hubert Dreyfus, a philosopher at Berkeley whose notes on *Being and Time* have just been published and have been long awaited, and whose early book *What Computers Can't Do* was another strong and powerful influence on me. That's a great book, both in its first and second editions. Through my friendship with Dreyfus, who is a magnificent teacher, and because of the pleasure and illumination I gained from his courses, there is probably some kind of Heidegger-Wittgensteinian circuit (there *is* a relationship, though a tortured one, between Heidegger and Wittgenstein) that has had more power in my work than I consciously acknowledge. Therefore, I guess I end up saying that in a way Reed may be right.

Olson: Last October, over dinner, you and I discussed various issues with Dinesh D'Souza, and I remember your eloquent and impassioned plea for him to believe that feminism is "the real thing," that significant and substantial developments are occurring within and because of feminism. Exactly what of importance is happening in feminism?

Fish: I couldn't answer that question because feminism has become as a discipline and a series of disciplines so complicated, such a map with so many different city-states or nation-states, that it would be foolish of me to start pronouncing. What I was trying to convey to Dinesh (the question of whether or not one conveys *anything* to Dinesh is an interesting one) is that the questions raised by feminism, because they were questions raised not in the academy but in the larger world and that then made their way into the academy, have energized more thought and social action than any other "ism" in the past twenty or thirty years, including Marxism, which may have been in that position in an earlier period but is in our present culture no longer in that position. Now what is that position? It is the position that in my view marks the true power of a form of inquiry or thought: when the assumptions encoded in the vocabulary of a form of thought become inescapable in the larger society. For example, people who have never read a feminist tract and would be alarmed at the thought of reading one are nevertheless being influenced by feminist thinking in ways of which they are unaware or are to some extent uncomfortably aware. Such influence often exhibits itself in the form of resistance: "*I'm* not going to fall in with any of that feminist crap," thereby falling in

headfirst as it were. My benchmark comparison here is with Freudianism. Freudianism's influence on our society is absolutely enormous
and in the same way. People who have never read Freud, and who
would not think of reading Freud, nevertheless have a ready store of
Freudian concepts about the unconscious, repression, slips of the
tongue, a vague sense that there's something called the "Oedipus
Complex," and so on. *That's* when a form of thought has genuine
power; it becomes unavoidable in our society. Feminism, I think, has
that status and will continue to have that status (especially if there are
more things like the Clarence Thomas/Anita Hill hearings).

Olson: You have argued that "feminists who rely in their arguments on
a distinction between male and female epistemologies are wrong, but,
nevertheless, it may not be wrong (in the sense of unproductive) for
them to rely on it." Currently, the most influential version of feminism
in composition is concerned primarily with such a distinction. Would
you explain, first, why such a distinction is problematic, and also how
it nonetheless might be productive?

Fish: Well, it's problematic in relation to my own notion of the way belief
and conviction work. My stricture on that particular piece of feminist
theory follows from my general position on critical self-consciousness. Critical self-consciousness, which was my main object of attack
for a number of years (now I see that the true object of attack all along
was liberalism in general), is the idea that you can in some way step
back from, rise above, get to the side of your beliefs and convictions
so that they will have less of a hold on you than they would had you not
performed this distancing action, thereby enabling you to survey the
field of possibilities relatively unencumbered by the beliefs and
convictions whose hold has been relaxed. This seems to me to be *zany*
because it simply assumes but never explains an ability to perform that
distancing act, never pausing to identify that ability and to link the
possession of that ability with the thesis that usually begins discussions
that lead to this point—the thesis of the general historicity of all human
efforts. That is, most people who come to the point of talking about
critical self-consciousness or reflective equilibrium or being aware of
the status of one's own discourse are also persons who believe strongly
in the historical and socially constructed nature of reality; but somehow, at a certain moment in the argument, they are able to marry this
belief in social constructedness with a belief in the possibility of
stepping back from what has been socially constructed or stepping
back from one's own self. I don't know how they manage this. I think,

in fact, that they manage it by not recognizing the contradiction.

The feminist version of this, at least in the strain of feminism to which you were referring, is to identify the ability to step back and not be gripped in a strong and almost military way by one's convictions, to identify that softer relationship to one's beliefs as "feminine" while perceiving the aggressive assertion of one's beliefs as "masculine." Well, if I'm right about the impossibility in a strong sense of that stepping back, then there could not be such a distinction between ways of knowing. There could be, however, as I do go on to say in that essay, different *styles* in relation to which one's beliefs are held and urged and introduced to others. And those different styles will have different effects, although, again, contingent on particular situations. It's not always the case that proceeding in a soft and relatively mild way to forward a point of view will produce effect X while a brusk and peremptory declaration of one's point of view will produce effect Y. It depends. I like to think of these not so much as a difference in female and male ways of knowing but a difference in modes of aggression. So, finally, it's whether or not you favor or at the moment find useful garden-variety aggressiveness, or whether you take refuge in passive aggressiveness—which can often be the most aggressive form of aggressiveness. This is the difference often at the root of these discussions, and it also gets into discussions of collaborative learning and of attempts to decenter classroom authority.

Olson: You just mentioned your distaste for liberalism . . .

Fish: Yes, I never tire of it.

Olson: I remember your saying not long ago that you see conservatives today as behaving "like a bunch of thugs" and liberals as "foolish and silly," but given a choice between the two, you'd side with silliness over thuggishness. You've been openly contemptuous of liberals, both within the field and in society at large. What is it about the liberal intellectual agenda that you find so repugnant?

Fish: What distresses me about liberalism is that it is basically a brief against belief and conviction. I understand its historical origins in a weariness with theological battles that were in the sixteenth and seventeenth centuries and earlier (and still today in parts of the world) real battles: people bled, died, mutilated one another, and so on. As every historian has told us for many years, the passions of seventeenth-century sectarian wars, especially in England, led to a sense of weariness, to a lack of faith in the ability of persons ever to be reconciled on these points, and therefore to a desire to diminish their centrality to one's life. That's one of the sources, not the only source, of liberalism's appeal. Liberalism takes the inescapable reality of contending agendas or of points of view or, as we would now say in a shorthand way, of "difference" and tries to find an overarching procedural structure which will accommodate difference and will at least defer the pressure to decide in a final way between strongly differing points of view. Liberalism is a way not so much to avoid conflict (because liberalism is born out of the unhappy insight that conflict cannot be avoided) but to contain it, to manage it, and therefore to find some form of human association in which difference can be accommodated and persons can be allowed the practice and even cultivation of their points of view, but in which the machinery of the state will not prefer one point of view to another but will in fact produce structures that will ensure that contending points of view can coexist in the same space without coming to a final conflict.

The difficulty with this view is that it assumes that structures of a kind that are neutral between contending agendas can in fact be fashioned. What I wish to say, and I'm certainly not the only one or by any means the first one to say it, is that *any* structure put in place is *necessarily* one that favors some agendas, usually by acts of recognition or nonrecognition, at the expense of others. That is, any organization that one sets up already is based on some implicit ordering of possible courses of action that have been identified or recognized as being within the pale. Then there are other kinds of actions that are simply not recognized and are therefore, as it were, written out of the program before the beginning. Now, this has not been a *conscious* act because for it to have been a conscious act it would have to have been produced in the very realm of reflective self-consciousness that I am always denying. Nevertheless, it is an inescapable fact about organization, from my point of view. So what liberalism does in the *guise* of devising structures that are neutral between contending agendas is to produce a structure that is far from neutral but then, by virtue of a political success, has claimed the right to think of itself as neutral. What this then means is that in the vocabulary of liberalism certain kinds of words mark the zone of suspicion—words like *conviction*, *belief*, *passion*, all of which are for the liberal mentality very close to fanaticism.

You could have noted a nice instance of this in the Gulf War frenzy of 1990 and 1991 when the charge that was made again and again about Saddam Hussein and his followers was that they *believed* something so strongly that they wouldn't "listen to reason." The February 1991 issue of *The New Republic* was devoted largely to the situation on campus but had three or four essays on the still-evolving Gulf War situation, and it became quite clear that for the editors and writers of *The New Republic* the danger represented by Saddam Hussein and the danger represented by multiculturalism or ethnic studies were exactly the same danger. This was the danger of persons passionately committed to an agenda, a set of assumptions—on the one hand a bunch of nutty Iraqis and on the other hand a bunch of nutty English teachers. In both cases, the obvious and compelling power of reason and rationality somehow had been overwhelmed by passion and conviction. In a way, liberalism, under this description, could be seen as a post-eighteenth-century variation of an old Judeo-Christian account of the nature of man in which man is composed of two parts: willful, irrational passion on the one hand and on the other hand something still residing in the breast, that spark of true intuition left us after the fall. So in many Christian homiletic traditions, human life is imagined as a battleground between the carnal self controlled by its appetites and something else, often called "conscience" or the "word of God," within. Now what happens in the Enlightenment is that the theological moorings of this view are detached, and in place of things like the conscience or the memory of God or the image of God's love, one has Reason. But in the older tradition (and here's the big difference), that which was contending with the carnal, because it was identified with the divine, had an obvious teleological valance to it. You take away that and substitute for it Reason and then you have something as your supposed lodestar which, by the Enlightenment's definition of Reason, is independent of value. It seems to me that out of this many of the problems of liberalism, as described by a great many people, arise. So I think that liberalism is an incoherent notion born out of a correct insight that we'll never see an end to these squabbles and that therefore we must do something, and the doing something is somehow to find a way to rise above the world of conviction, belief, passion. I simply don't think that's possible.

Olson: What would be an intellectual agenda that is *not* silly or thuggish?

Fish: I'm a localist, which is already almost a dangerous thing to say. By that I mean I don't have an intellectual agenda in any strong sense, or to put it in deliberately provocative terms: I don't have any principles. If I believe in anything, I believe in rules of thumb, in the sense that in any tradition there are certain kinds of aphorisms or axioms which encode that tradition's values, purposes, and goals; and people who are deeply embedded in that tradition are in some sense, often below the threshold of self-consciousness, committed to those values, purposes, and goals which, however, *can* in the course of the history of a tradition or profession, change. Therefore, as I say quite often (and it's true) my forward time span is generally two hours. By that I mean I tend not to think about or worry about anything more in the future than two hours hence. From a negative point of view, one might characterize my vision, therefore, as severely constrained and limited. I walk into a situation and there's something wrong sometimes, but my sense of what is wrong is very much attached to the local moment, the resources within that moment that might be available to remedy the wrong, and the possibility that my own actions might in some way contribute to that remedy. Then if someone starts commenting, "You act this way in situation *A* and three weeks ago in situation *B* I saw you act in ways that would under a general philosophical description be thought of as a contradiction," I answer, "Don't bother me. Give me a break. I am not in the business of organizing my successive actions so that they all conform to or are available to a coherent philosophical account." A lot of people assume that this is what action in the world should be: you strive from some mode of action that, if viewed from outside over a period of time, would be seen as consistent in philosophical terms. Again, I don't see that. That seems to me to go along with the fetishization of the unified self and a whole lot of other things that as "postmodernists" we are supposedly abandoning but that keep returning with a vengeance.

Olson: In *Doing What Comes Naturally*, you discuss at length the role of "intention" in the production and reception of discourse. As a check on both those who "ignore" authorial intention as well as those who defer to it, you explain that "there is only one way to read or interpret, and that is the way of intention. But to read intentionally is not to be constrained relative to some other (nonexistent) way of reading." You say this is so because any meaning is "thinkable only in the light of an intentional structure already assumed." Would you elaborate on the nature and role of "intentional structure"?

Fish: Sure. I would back off for a moment and consider what the alternative picture would be. The alternative picture would be intention as something added on to a meaningful structure. In other words, those people who wish either to avoid or ignore intention believe that it is possible to speak of the meaning of something independently of a purposeful human action. I do not so believe. Another way to put this is that linguists (some linguists, not all) often talk about what words mean "in the language" as opposed to what they might mean in particular situations. I don't believe that the category "in the language" has any content whatsoever. I do believe, of course, in dictionaries and in grammars or accounts of grammar, but I always assume that dictionaries and accounts of grammar are being written from within the assumption of a range of possible human intentions as realized in particular situations, and that the fact that this range of possible human intentions as realized in particular situations is not on the surface, is not a part of the surface accounts of words given in a dictionary or in a grammar, is simply to be explained by the deep assumption of intentionality which is so deeply assumed that some people think they can in some particular situations get along without it. I always say to my students, "Just try to imagine uttering a sentence that is meaningful and, not as an afterthought but already in the act of thinking up such a sentence, imagine some intentional situation—that is, a situation with an agent with a purpose in relation to the configurations of the world that he or she wishes in some way to alter or announce—imagine doing without that and I say that you won't be able to." It's always the case that when you're attempting to determine what something means, what you are attempting to do is to penetrate to, to identify the intention of, some purposeful agent.

Now having said that, what methodological consequences follow? The answer is "none whatsoever," because (this is usually my favorite answer to almost any question) having now been persuaded that to construe meaning is also to identify intentional behavior, you are in no better position to go forward than you were before because all the problems remain. You must yourself decide what you mean by an "agent." Are you talking about the "liberal individual" formulating thoughts in his or her mind? Are you talking about the agency of a "community," of a group in *my* sense, or of a paradigm member, in Kuhn's sense? Are you talking, in an older intellectual tradition of the history of ideas, of the *Zeitgeist*—the spirit of an age within whose intentional structure everyone writes? Or in theological terms are you talking of a tradition in which my hand held the pen but it was the spirit of the Lord that moved me—a tradition I myself in no way denigrate? These are not decisions to which you will be helped by having decided that the construal of meaning is inseparable from the stipulation of intention. You then will also have to decide what is evidence for the intention that you finally stipulate, and that too is a question that was as wide open and as difficult before you came upon the gospel of intentionalism as it is now that you *have* come upon the gospel of intentionalism. So for shorthand purposes and in terms that most of your readers and mine would recognize, E.D. Hirsch was right when he asserted the primacy of intention back in 1960 and 1967, and he was simply wrong to think that having done so he had provided a methodological key or any kind of method whatsoever. This is also the argument, made brilliantly in my view, of Knapp and Michaels' essay "Against Theory."

Olson: In "Going Down the Anti-Formalist Road" you write, "There is no such thing as literal meaning, if by literal meaning one means a meaning that is perspicuous no matter what the context and no matter what is in the speaker's or hearer's mind, a meaning that because it is prior to interpretation can serve as a constraint on interpretation." You conclude, "Meanings that seem perspicuous and literal are rendered so by forceful interpretive acts and not by the properties of language." Exactly what is a "forceful interpretive act"? What lends it its "force"?

Fish: A forceful interpretive act needn't be committed or performed by any one person; in fact, usually it is not, except in extraordinary cases. The forceful interpretive act takes place over time, and the agencies involved in it are multiple. Its effects are more easily identified than the process that leads to them. The effects are the production of a situation in which for all competent members of a community the utterance of certain words will be understood in an absolutely uniform way. That *does* happen. It is a possible historical contingent experience. When that happens you have, as far as I'm concerned, a linguistic condition that it might be perfectly appropriate to characterize as the condition of literalism. That is, at that moment you can with some justice say that these words, when uttered in this community, will mean only this one thing. The mistake is to think that it is the property of the words that produces this rather than a set of uniform interpretive assumptions that so fill the minds and consciousness of members that they will, upon receiving a certain set of words, immediately hear them in a certain way. Of course, that can always be upset by a variety of mechanisms, but it need not be upset; this condition can last a long, long, long time.

I'll tell you a story I've told many times. When my daughter was six years old, we were sitting at the dinner table one evening. We then had two small black dachshunds. My daughter Susan was doing something with the dachshunds under the table, and it was experienced at least by me as disruptive. So I said to her, "Susan, stop playing with the dachshunds." She held up her hands in a kind of "Look, Dad, no hands" gesture and said, "I'm not *playing* with the dachshunds." So I said, "Susan, stop *kicking* the dachshunds." She turned my attention to the soft motions of her feet and said, "I'm not *kicking* the dachshunds." So I said, forgetting every lesson I had ever learned as a so-called philosopher of language, "Susan don't do *anything* with the dachshunds!" She replied, "You mean I don't have to feed them anymore?" At that moment I knew several things. First, I knew I was in a drama called "the philosopher and the dupe" and that she was the philosopher and I was the dupe. I also knew that this was a game that she could continue to play indefinitely because she could always recontextualize what she understood to be the context of my question in such a way as to destabilize the literalness on which I had been depending, which she too—within the situation of the dinner table, our relationship, our house—recognized in as literal a way as I did. That story, which can be unfolded endlessly, encapsulates for me this set of issues that you were asking about.

Olson: In your essay on critical self-consciousness, you take issue first with Stephen Toulmin because he "advocates self-conscious reflection on one's own beliefs as a way to neutralize bias immediately after having asserted the unavailability of the 'objective standpoint' that would make such reflection a possible achievement." Then you criticize the tradition of critical self-consciousness on the left as being "frankly political," as "rigorously and relentlessly negative, intent always on exposing or unmasking those arrangements of power that present themselves in reason's garb." Finally, you pronounce the critical project "a failure." Granting your argument that we are never free of constraints and therefore there never are truly free actions, would you not agree that the project of critical self-consciousness—whether conservative or radical—is nonetheless productive and beneficial, that we'd be poorer without it?

Fish: No. I do not agree because I sense you venturing into the regulative ideal territory—that is, we can never do this but it's a good thing to try. The bad poetic version of this is given in a line (that's even bad for him) by Browning (in my view the worst major poet): "A man's reach should exceed his grasp or what's a heaven for?" That is really the philosophy or point of view behind regulative ideal arguments, whether they're Kantian or Habermasian or any other "ian." I have no truck with them;

I just don't see their point. It's just a form of idealism.

Olson: Sure, it's idealistic to think that we can be truly self-conscious in a critical way, but doesn't the process of trying to get there turn out to be productive?

Fish: It depends on what you mean by "the process of trying to get there." You may be surprised or even distressed to hear this, but there is about to be published another Fish/Dworkin debate. I participated last year in a conference at Virginia, Pragmatism in Law and Society, which was in some ways appropriately centered on the work of Richard Rorty. The organizer, a professor of political science, assembled a really interesting cast of characters to speak about these questions. A few weeks before the conference, I received what I thought was a strange call from the convener of the conference who said that Ronald Dworkin wished to know which of the participants in the conference were going to write about him and what they were going to say. I said *I* wasn't going to write about him, that I was writing about Posner and Rorty, which I did. What I didn't know at the time is that for some reason Dworkin had been asked to be a commentator on the proceedings. His idea of being a commentator was to find out what essays would be directed either wholly or partly at him so that he could in the G.E. Moore tradition write a reply to his critics yet again. I would have seemed to have, at least with respect to me, foiled this intention because I didn't say *anything* about Dworkin. But when Dworkin came to write his commentary on the conference papers, he ignored this small difficulty and simply picked up the threads of earlier quarrels as if I *had* written my paper on him. When I saw that, I became distressed, and so I wrote a reply to Dworkin.

Now, Dworkin was arguing against the "theory has no consequences" position and for critical self-consciousness and for critically reflective stances on one's own assumptions—for a strong relationship, in short, between critical theory and practice. He chose as his example (this was a huge mistake) Ted Williams. Ted Williams was my hero as a boy. I had carried a picture of him around in my wallet for many years until it just fell apart. What Dworkin said was, as a kind of knock-down argument in his view, "The greatest hitter of modern baseball built a theory before every pitch." His source for this was Ted's book, *The Science of Hitting*. I got the latest edition of *The Science of Hitting*, read it carefully, annotated it, and pointed out several things. First of all, in *The Science of Hitting* Ted has an account of Ty Cobb's theory of hitting which he examines in detail—Cobb thought this and thought that in relation to velocity, to the way the foot moved, what you did with the bat, and so forth. Then after doing this, Ted absolutely demolishes it. He says, in effect, that what Cobb was advising is not possible for the human body to perform. Five pages later, Ted describes Cobb quite reasonably as the greatest hitter in baseball history. The conclusion is inescapable: the greatest hitter in baseball history had a theory of how he did it which had no relationship whatsoever, and could not have had any relationship, to what he did. Ted then goes on in another section of the book to describe what he thinks of as the mode of action of a great hitter. He goes on to hypothetical (but not really hypothetical; you have a sense that he's reconstructing moments in his own career) accounts of what a good hitter is doing as he stands up at the plate. What a good hitter is doing, according to Ted, is thinking things like this: "Well, last time he threw me a fast ball and there were two men on base and it was the fourth inning; now it's the eighth inning and there's no one on base but the score is four to three; I know that he doesn't like to rely on his fast ball so much in the later innings, and so forth and so on." Now what can one say about thoughts like that? First, one wants to say that they're highly self-conscious. They're self-conscious in the sense that there is a definite reflection not only on the present moment of activity but on the relationship between the present moment of activity and past moments which are now being "self-consciously" recalled. However, my point is that this self-consciousness really is not another level of practice but in fact is, how shall I describe it, itself a component in practice and that what Ted was saying to the would-be hitter was something like, "Be attentive to all dimensions of the situation." Now, is there a separate capacity called the "being attentive capacity" or what we might call the "critically reflective capacity"? Answer: No. Is it the case that you can develop a muscle or a pineal gland or something such that you could in any variety of different situations involving different forms of action activate that muscle? The answer is no. What you in fact do, when you do it well, is become *attentive* to the situation. The shape of your attentiveness is situation specific and dependent, so that—returning to your question—insofar as one is ever critically reflective, one is critically reflective *within* the routines of a practice. One's critical reflectiveness is in fact a function of, its shape is a function of, the routines of the practice. What most people want from critical reflectiveness is precisely a distance on the practice rather than what we might call a heightened degree of attention while performing in the practice. I haven't given you the argument as elegantly as I gave it in my reply to Dworkin. I guess in the end what I would want to say is that insofar as critical self-consciousness is a possible human achievement, it requires no special ability and cannot be cultivated as an independent value apart from particular situations: it's simply being normally reflective. It's not an abnormal, special—that is, *theoretical*—capacity. Insofar as the demand is for it to be such—that is, special, abnormal—it is a demand that can never be fulfilled.

Olson: In "Profession Despise Thyself" you say that we in literary studies have made ourselves "fair game" to criticism "by subscribing to views of our enterprise in relation to which our activities can only be either superfluous or immoral ("How can you study Milton while the Third World starves?")." Noam Chomsky has said in *JAC* that he does not find most academic questions "humanly significant," suggesting that to be humanly useful academics should devote some of their time to social activism. Do you believe we in English studies should turn our attention to more socially useful activities?

Fish: I think it depends. English studies cannot itself be made into a branch of inquiry that has direct and immediate social and political payoffs, at least not in the way the United States is now structured. In other countries and other traditions, it would have been more possible for there to be a direct connection between literary activity and social and political activity, and perhaps in some transformation of our society that has not yet occurred it could be the case that the kinds of analyses we're performing in class could have an immediate impact on the larger social and economic questions being debated in society. As for the question (which I now will understand in a way that Chomsky would probably find trivial), "Should English teachers devote their energies to social causes?" my answer is, "Why not?" It's like *pro bono* work in the legal world: you decide what it is you're interested in doing, working in political ways, in social ways, and you volunteer. In a way, what Chomsky is saying is very congenial to the academic mentality— a mentality that has a deep interest in diminishing its own value. Just why this is so is worthy of many pages of analysis. The academic generally participates in the devaluation of his or her own activities to a much greater degree than the practitioners in other fields do. It seems to me that academic activity is a human activity. As a human activity, like any other activity, it has its constraints and therefore its areas of possible effectivity as well as many areas in which it will not be effective because it will not touch them. This makes it no better or no worse on some absolute scale (that doesn't exist) than any other human activity. However, at a particular moment in history a legitimate question is, "Do we want to put our energies in this human activity that has this structure of plus and minus in terms of gains and losses and opportunities, or this one?" That's a perfectly reasonable question to ask as long as one doesn't think that one is asking a question that has a Platonic structure, in the old sense, or a surface/deep structure opposition, in the Chomskian sense. I'm temperamentally opposed to those who wish to regard the academic life as an inferior, unauthentic form of human activity. It's *another* form of human activity. It should neither be privileged—as some romantic humanists privilege it so that only those who "live the life of the mind" are really living—nor should it be denigrated as the area of the trivial in relation to which getting one's hands authentically dirty is the true counterweight. I think both of those characterizations are bankrupt.

Olson: In *Doing What Comes Naturally*, you speculate that the immense popularity of books like E.D. Hirsch's and Allan Bloom's signal that "the *public* fortunes of rationalist-foundationalist thought have taken a favorable turn": "One can expect administrators and legislators to propose reforms (and perhaps even purges) based on Bloom's arguments (the rhetorical force of anti-rhetoricalism is always being revived)." Do you predict massive (and counterproductive) state intervention in the educational system?

Fish: The current political situation (by "current" I mean at this moment) suggests that that would be an unhappily canny prediction. Secretary of Education Lamar Alexander is poised to implement some of the ideas he inherited from William Bennett and which are being given continuing vitality in the administration's thinking by Lynne Cheney, as advised by people like Chester Finn and Diane Ravitch, among others. In all of these instances, the tendency is to label as disruptive and subversive—almost in a sense that returns us to the 1950s—all forms of thought that question the availability of transcendental standards and objective lines of measurement so that these forms of thought are regarded by the persons that I have named not as possible contenders in an arena of philosophical discussion but as Trojan horses of evil, decay, destruction of community, and so on. So long as these persons hold important positions in the government, positions connected to the administration of the educational world and the dispensation of funds, I think we do face a period in which there will be (at least on the national level, and in some cases on local levels) moves to curtail and purge. We're already seeing this in the activities of organizations like the National Association of Scholars and in the extensive network of student journalism that began with the *Dartmouth Review* but that has now extended far beyond the confines of Hanover, New Hampshire, allied with a number of prominently placed journalists in the national news media: people like Dorothy Rabinowitz and David Brooks of the *Wall Street Journal*; Jonathan Yardley at the *Post*; Charles Krauthammer and John Leo; political/popular writers like Dinesh D'Souza, Roger Kimball, and Charles Sykes; Nat Hentoff at the *Village Voice*—a whole series of people who can be relied upon to be mouthpieces for this very neo-conservative political agenda which is backed by huge amounts of right-wing foundation money provided by William Simon and others. I think that's a real force at the moment and a force to which many in the academy are only just now waking up.

Olson: You said we should be socially active. What measures can we take to prevent such reactionary trends?

Fish: The MLA panel I'm about to attend is entitled "Answering Back." Though I'm not a member of the panel, I'll be in the audience and I think we *must* talk back. I think that academics too often disdain communication with people outside the academic world and believe that attempting to speak to the public must necessarily be a diminution of our normal mode of discourse and that in order to speak to the public we must gear down and simplify our usual nuanced perspectives. In fact, I know from experience that speaking to the general public is indeed a task equally complex and difficult, but *differently* complex and difficult, as speaking to one's peers in learned journals or at conferences. There is a set of problems of translation and rhetorical accommodation that one comes upon when attempting to talk to audiences outside the academy which is absolutely fascinating and difficult. So unless we set our mind to this task, the capturing of the media pages and airwaves will continue as it has continued in the past year and a half so that up until four or five months ago it was difficult to find a view widely published *other* than the view being put forward by what we might call "Cheney and Company."

Olson: Certainly you have had your share of critics and detractors from both the left and the right. Are there any criticisms or misunderstandings of your work that you'd like to take issue with at this time? Anything to set straight?

Fish: No, not in any sense that hasn't been attempted before. As I say in *Doing What Comes Naturally* and elsewhere, there are basically two criticisms of my work; they come from the right and the left. The criticism from the right is that in arguing for notions like interpretive communities, the inescapability of interpretation, the infinite revisability of interpretive structures, I am undoing the fabric of civilization and opening the way to nihilist anarchy. The objection from the left is that I'm *not* doing that sufficiently. My argument to both is that on the one hand the fear that animates right-wing attacks on me is an unrealizable fear because one can never be divested of certainties and programs for action unless one believed that the mind itself could function as a calculating agent independently of the beliefs and convictions which supposedly we're going to lose; and on the other hand (or on the same hand), therefore, a program in which our first task is to divest ourselves of all our old and hegemonically imposed convictions in order to move forward to some new and braver world is an impossible task. On the one hand, hearkening to me will not lead to the decay of civilization, and on the other hand hearkening to me will not lead to the canonization of the status quo. In fact, on *these* kinds of points—and this is what most of my critics find most difficult to understand—hearkening to me will lead to *nothing*. Hearkening to me, from my point of view, is *supposed to* lead to nothing. As I say in *Doing What Comes Naturally* in answer to the question "What is the point?" the point is that there *is* no point, no yield of a positive programmatic kind to be carried away from these analyses. Nevertheless, *that* point (that there is no point) *is* the point because it's the promise of such a yield—either in the form of some finally successful identification of a foundational set of standards or some program by which we can move away from standards to ever-expanding liberation—it's the unavailability of such a yield that *is* my point, and therefore it would be contradictory for me to have a point beyond *that* point. People absolutely go bonkers when they hear that, but that's the way it is.

Chapter 5

From Multiculturalism to Academic Freedom: The Case against Universalism

The interview in chapter 4 was conducted in 1991. In the decade that intervened between then and the interview in this chapter, Fish substantially expanded the scope of his critical inquiry, probing a number of public, political, and legal issues that have relevance well beyond the confines of literary studies. One result of these efforts has been that an even greater audience began to identify him as an important public intellectual, and his role in American intellectual life expanded exponentially. Nevertheless, as he says below, he still does not think of himself as a "public intellectual," someone to whom the public regularly looks for insight on a range of substantive issues. He feels that the commentators who deserve that appellation interact with the larger public much more frequently than he does and opine on a broader range of subjects.

Despite the expansion of topics that Fish now writes about, all of his work—be it an analysis of Milton's *Areopagitica*, the development of reader-response criticism, or a meditation on the theory and application of the First Amendment—is animated by certain common concerns, the most significant being his rejection of attempts to establish general principles that apply to a subject independent of specific contexts. For example, he argues vigorously that there is no *general* category of hate speech. If hate speech and racism were truly abstract or universal categories, then any rational person would be able to recognize instances of them; however, argues Fish, the fact is that most people who utter hate speech or racist epithets would not describe their speech as hateful or racist. They would, in fact, describe themselves as uttering "the truth." For Fish, attempting to construct elaborate ways to define, capture, or universalize such speech is a quixotic endeavor, doomed from the start. A much more productive way of approaching the subject is to think of hate speech as "what your enemy says." That is, racism and hate speech are the names of rationalities that you loathe; rather than try to construct definitional standards that apply in all instances, and rather than try to "persuade" racists that they are misguided, we should, advises Fish, simply seek to use whatever power we have to *defeat* them.

As an example, he cites the case of David Irving, the Holocaust denier. When a well-publicized lawsuit thrust Irving into the public eye, St. Martin's Press withdrew plans to publish his next book. Far from being an infringement of Irving's First Amendment rights as many liberals argued (because, after all, no law was passed banning his books), this action was a perfect example, according to Fish, of how hateful speech can be successfully opposed. While it would have been unconstitutional to pass a law banning someone's books, acting in such a way as to "stifle, suppress, embarrass, and stigmatize those whose words and writings you think to be dangerous" is, says Fish, "a perfectly good and all-American activity."

This argument is closely related to Fish's discussion of academic freedom, and he in fact draws on Holocaust denial as an exemplary case because it puts the question of academic freedom into sharp focus. The typical discussions of academic freedom insist that it is necessary to give Holocaust deniers (particularly those with academic credentials) a "fair hearing." Fish points out that the original concept of academic freedom as defined by the AAUP in 1915 contrasts sharply with our more contemporary way of defining it. Far from being a *philosophical* concept premised on "the search for truth," academic freedom was a *political* concept aimed at "protecting the autonomy of the guild from trustees." That is, for its originators, academic freedom meant the freedom of academics "to order their own business and to weed out their own incompetents." This original sense of academic freedom is much more in keeping with Fish's own philosophical orientation because it derives not from large, philosophical, and abstract principles; it arises instead from the actual ways that specific work gets done in particular contexts.

Another form of universalism that Fish addresses is apparent in appeals to multiculturalism. He distinguishes between "boutique multiculturalism," which amounts to a mere appreciation and surface acceptance of different cultures (enjoying ethnic cuisines, music, art), and "strong multiculturalism," which represents a commitment to fostering the conditions in which a multiplicity of cultures can flourish. He suggests that while most strong multiculturalists have a moral investment in cultural pluralism, they will stop being strong multiculturalists "somewhat later than a boutique multiculturalist will stop being a multiculturalist" once they discover at the heart of a culture "an action or a moral attitude that they themselves cannot abide." That is, most multiculturalists—strong or weak—have a "substantive kicker" up their sleeves, a point beyond which they will not go in their acceptance of another culture; and, ironically, often that aspect of the culture will be central to the culture's identity or belief system. Thus, concludes Fish, multiculturalism is not a coherent notion. While the empirical fact of multiculturalism (we are living in an increasingly pluralistic world) is undisputable, "making a religion out of it" is pointless.

To some readers, Fish's arguments against the universal, the theoretical, and the "principled" amount to a defense of relativism, a charge that he has been denying since the 1970s. He insists that relativism is not the kind of "behavior that anyone could instantiate or perform because it would require that you hold your own views in an indifferent mix with the views of others and have no special commitment to them." He explains that people confuse relativism with the belief that there is no neutral perspective from which disputes between well-informed antagonists can be adjudicated, but this belief does not suggest that there are no truths or facts. That is, to argue that there are no mechanisms available for settling disputes with certainty is quite different from arguing that there are no truths or facts.

Perhaps what is most frustrating to many readers is Fish's typical rhetorical maneuver of first demonstrating how a certain principle or law or theory or assumption does not hold up to a certain kind of analysis, and then announcing that his analysis should not be construed as an argument for abandoning or even revising it. Fish states vehemently, however, that he is not in the business of producing outcomes. In fact, he insists that "if after having read me or heard me you go away with something useful, I will have failed"—that is, he will have fallen into the same epistemological trap that he accuses others of falling into. He maintains that his aim is not to produce change; rather, it is simply to demonstrate that those who are making the reverse arguments are wrong: "I'm just pointing out that they're wrong." Since so many people are "wrong," Fish doesn't anticipate running out of things to say for quite a long time.

While Fish has certainly made an indelible mark on intellectual history, he is most proud of his work as a literary critic. He sees his lasting legacy as his contribution to English studies: the numerous essays and books on such authors as Milton, Herbert, Donne, Marvell, Jonson, Burton, and Bacon—many of which are "still doing work in their fields." He believes that the one advantage he has over many of his peers—at least so far as his critical legacy is concerned—is the accessibility of his writing: readers do not find it necessary to "learn an entirely new vocabulary" in order to comprehend his work. Of course, the exact extent and duration of Fish's legacy will remain a question for future generations to answer, but one thing is certain: he has clearly animated the intellectual life of both English studies and the larger academic community with his wit, cogency, sagacity, and perspicuity, inspiring a generation of scholars, teachers, and even non-academics who care deeply about the profound and mystifying dynamics of rhetoric, interpretation, and epistemology.

ザ   ザ   ザ

Olson: A decade ago, I asked you if you considered yourself a writer. Since then, you've written several books that appeal to a mass audience. Do you still think of yourself as a writer?

Fish: Yes, I think of myself as a writer, and as I may have said the last time we talked, everything for me centers on the sentence. I derive a great deal of pleasure when I come across a sentence, written by anyone, that seems well-turned or to do its job. I've found that in a lot of writing—not only academic writing, but in a lot of writing these days—there's not much of an ability to handle sentences crisply. I just admire that, as I assume watchmakers admire certain things about the movements of fine timepieces, and it's with this same kind of appreciation of "craft" that I think about a lot of things in general. It always impresses and pleases me (it's almost a combination of aesthetic and moral pleasure) when I see someone who is doing his or her job well. He or she knows what the job is about and performs it well. And this could be anything: you may walk into a restaurant and get a sense that the people there are able to command their profession and to perform its obligations almost effortlessly and in a way that you hadn't noticed until you started comparing it with all the other, unhappy experiences you've had in restaurants. Or it might be the way someone drives a car, or the way a commercial enterprise is operated.

Olson: When we last talked, you described your writing process as somewhat traditional. You did not use a computer, and you rarely revised. How has your writing process changed in the last decade?

Fish: My writing process has changed in that I now use a computer; that's the big change. I had two New Year's resolutions that I actually kept (I think it was in 1997). I don't recall any other occasion when I kept a New Year's resolution. One was to finish a Milton book that I had been working on since 1973. The other was to get online. I did them both, in part because I had a semester that spring at the National Humanities Center in Research Park, North Carolina that allowed me to write a very lengthy introductory chapter of close to a hundred pages. I decided I would do it on this new instrument that I had gotten. I had the usual kinds of entry-level problems, but they all passed and now I'm just like anybody else.

It is true that I don't revise much. I write a couple of pages a day, except when I reach a point where everything seems to be unfolding. This happened actually last week. I was writing a paper on academic freedom and Holocaust denial for a conference later this fall. I wrote perhaps seven or eight pages last Sunday and then finished it off. But that's very unusual.

Olson: Aside from *How Milton Works*, much of your recent work has addressed a large, general audience. How do you envision your audience when you are writing?

Fish: I envision my audience as made up of people who are well educated, in the sense that they're accustomed to reading materials that are about substantive and perhaps even philosophical issues, but who may not be professionally involved with those issues. Therefore, I always think of my audience as a group of persons who should be helped along, not because they are in any way deficient in intelligence or acumen but because they're not inside some of these topics in a professional manner. There's a difference between addressing that audience and, say, going to an American Association of Law Schools meeting and appearing on a panel about the First Amendment. You know that everybody in the audience can recite all of the cases just as you can and refers to them in shorthand, just as movie critics refer to movies in shorthand or Shakespeareans refer to "the Scottish play." That audience is a very specialized one. The audience that might read what I write in a magazine or in an op-ed piece in the *Times* is a different kind of audience in that you have to explain a bit more of the background context—not so that you can bring them up to speed, but so that you can make use of the intelligence they have by not putting them behind an eight ball from the very beginning.

Olson: Does the fact that lately you are addressing a general audience mean that you are transcending the role of what you call "the cameo intellectual" or "the rent for a day intellectual" and are becoming more of a "public intellectual"—someone to whom the public "regularly looks for illumination on any number of issues"?

Fish: I don't think so. I have a nice relationship with the *New York Times,* which asks me to do op-ed pieces more often than I'm able to do them. I don't come up with ideas that often, and sometimes when an idea is suggested to me, the topic doesn't strike me as something that I really have anything interesting to say about. I don't believe that I'm in the position of commentators like, let's say, Gary Wills or Christopher Hitchens or Dinesh D'Souza or others who are on National Public Radio and various panel talk shows all of the time. I'll do something like that perhaps two or three times a year. Maybe when a book comes out and there's a set of interviews there will be more appearances, but the people who I think are really deserving of the title "public intellectuals" are interacting with the larger public much more often than I am.

Olson: So frequency is the key then.

Fish: Frequency is one key. There's also the sense with people like Gary Wills and the others that I've named that there is a huge number of topics on which they might be commenting. I'm thinking of Norman Ornstein of the American Enterprise Institute and a whole bunch of people like that whose names are recognizable and whose expertise, at least as presented in their columns or magazine pieces, seems much wider than mine.

Olson: In the Preface to *How Milton Works*, you comment that your reading of Milton has not changed much in twenty-five years. One could say the same about your take on "principle" or on "theory." Yet, it clearly would be unfair to suggest that your thought has not developed over time. What changes do you feel your thinking has undergone over the years?

Fish: While I don't know what specific changes I could instance, I know what the change feels like. There are certain basic issues and questions that have animated my work, and they are the same ones in discussions of Milton and in the theory of the First Amendment. It's just that over the years my sense of how to deal with those issues has, I would hope, been refined. Some of the issues present themselves in the context of materials that I hadn't considered before, and I work through these materials and get a new take on some of the old positions. In fact, that's just what's happened with the Holocaust denial/academic freedom issue. I have written about academic freedom before, but I've never written about Holocaust denial. I hadn't really looked into it, except for the occasional newspaper pieces or television reports that everyone sees. So now I've taken my set of concerns and my positions and my theses about the relationship or non-relationship of theory and philosophy to practical everyday work and run it through the Holocaust-denial problem. Not surprisingly, it comes out in the end just about the same, but the arguments necessarily have a kind of new shape (or at least a perspectivally different shape) because the materials are very specific and not the materials that I've worked with before.

Olson: An article published in *Lingua Franca* not long ago suggested that you might not be entirely happy with your move from Duke to the deanship at the University of Illinois in Chicago. Do your administrative duties impinge substantially on your scholarly productivity?

Fish: I was the Slate diarist for a week, and I took that assignment in what I thought was the spirit of it, which is that they wanted something more personally reflective, or self-reflective, than I usually do. Other people—like my wife, for example—do that a lot. So I tried my best as I went through the days of the diary to get a sense of what I was thinking and feeling or fearing and so forth. I've been extremely pleased by this move. It's worked out very well.

Olson: So, your move hasn't affected your scholarly work.

Fish: No, actually not. That is, *The Trouble with Principle* was finished during the first half-year I was here. The Milton book was put together and revised extensively last spring. There have been several essays—such as the one on Holocaust denial, one on Herbert, and one on Marvell—that have now been published. I've written some other pieces in the legal arena, including one called "Theory Minimalism," which I quite like. So it goes on. The reason is that I've been fortunate all my life to be able to work efficiently. You know the phrase "to turn on a dime"? If there's an hour and I'm on a plane or in a train station, I'll pull out a couple of essays or articles or something that I know I need to work on and I will start planning something. I don't seem to need what a lot of people do need: that space of preparation where you get yourself ready to work, and the light has to be right, and there can't be noise, and so on. I've never had that problem. So I guess what it amounts to is that for me focusing is something that can happen almost instantaneously when I get the opportunity—you know, a little bit of time. It works out quite well that way.

Olson: Your main argument in *Professional Correctness* is that while some critics are attempting to transform literary study so that it is "more immediately engaged" with political issues such as oppression, racism, and cultural imperialism, so long as they make their points *as* literary critics "no one but a few of their friends will be listening." And you also argue that, conversely, if they address such issues in politically effective ways, they will no longer be acting as literary critics. I believe that this argument has been widely misunderstood. Some readers have read it as an argument against political activism; others have read it as an attack on progressive thought; still others have read it as a diatribe against cultural studies and as a reactionary attempt to move literary study back to an apolitical aestheticism. How do you respond to such readings

Fish: Let's take those in reverse order, beginning with the cultural studies fear. I am not arguing against cultural studies—that is, as an activity that can ask extremely interesting questions and use materials that hitherto hadn't been taken seriously to come up with new answers to those questions. The political claim that is added to the claim of cultural studies that I think is a correct one is that it provides new and illuminating perspectives on both familiar and unfamiliar materials. That I think is a claim that cultural studies can make good on. The claim *sometimes* made (". . . and by doing this we are striking a blow *for X* or *against Y*") seems to me, as I've said over and over again, bizarre, megalomaniacal, and one more instance of the odd wish of academics to be more than what their job description allows them to be. So that's the cultural studies argument.

As for being against progressive thought, that depends on what you mean by progressive thought. Certainly, in the context of the work that I've done both in straight literary studies and in theoretical work, I have often been attacked for being so on the edge or for being so outrageously outside of the bounds of ordinary thought, that it doesn't sound like I'm against progressive thought. I am, however, in general against that form of cognitive idealism that says that if we can only get our intellectual categories straight and in order, then we will be able to order, revolutionize, clean up, improve, and purify the world. I'm thinking, "What is this?! This does not make any sense." I'm going to have to write something about that this year. I'm finally going to write my second big anti-Habermas essay. I taught a course in political theory in the political science department in the spring, and one of the books I taught was the big, fat book of Habermas' (well, actually they're all big and fat), *Between Facts and Norms*, which is extremely rich in relation to the set of problems that he's working with. I saw more clearly than I had ever seen before that Habermas' call for, as he puts it, "an orientation toward understanding" is an exemplary instance of what's wrong with a certain supposedly idealized relationship between doing philosophical work and doing change in the world. To put it as simply as possible, there is *no* orientation toward understanding. There's an orientation toward understanding *within some perspectives*, some interested perspectives already informed by purpose, situation, and disciplinary, political, domestic, and social contexts. We are all oriented toward understanding in *those* contexts. There are many moments in our everyday lives, both professional and non-professional, when we pause and say to ourselves or to our interlocutor in a conversation, "Okay, let's figure out where we are, how we got here, what we can do to get to the place where we would like to go." And so, you've stopped doing things for a while, and you're trying to understand your situation so that you might act more effectively within it. But when Habermas talks about an "orientation toward understanding," he means "understanding" with a capital *U*, understanding without any particular contextual content—and there *ain't any such thing*. That's it, pure and simple. That's been my argument for years, and I'm kind of pleased that Habermas has made it so clear in this new book why his entire argument is, from the very word *go*, without coherence, sense, intelligibility, or interest.

Olson: You make the point in *Professional Correctness* that as a discipline literary criticism is characterized by a limited set of concerns and practices and that such concerns and practices are *constitutive* of the discipline—that if we were to replace such questions as "What does this poem mean?" with questions about, say, socio-economic inequities we would no longer be doing literary criticism. But surely all disciplines are susceptible to evolution, de-evolution, change. Is this not true of literary studies? Why can't we change the very concerns and practices that constitute literary studies? Why can't literary studies simply be redefined?

Fish: Why can't it simply be redefined? That's again a question that evokes a form of argument I always make, which is that you can't just get up in the morning and say, "Today, I will redefine the context of work within which I've been engaged." Or, "Today, I will become more open to new ideas." It doesn't happen that way. It's not a resolution of the will. You're embedded in a conversation, in a context, in a layered history that precedes you; and within that history (which now gives you your understanding of what the alternative courses of action might be) you can move here, you can move there, you can see possibilities of combining components of the enterprise, or you can see possibilities of turning the enterprise upside down or three-quarters of the way around, but that's a long way from just *deciding* that you're going to redefine it. If you decide you're going to redefine it, it's like saying, "We're not going to do this anymore; we're going to do something else"—which is fine and dandy, just don't call the "something else" by the same name that you used to call the "this," because it ain't "this" anymore, that's all.

I certainly believe that literary studies is continually evolving, but insofar as it defines itself as *literary* studies and not as sociology, economics, philosophy, law, macrame, grape picking or anything else, the change is always a change that has as its aim and purpose a new and better sense of what *literary* studies is. The key phrase in *Professional Correctness* is "the distinctiveness of tasks." Now, that distinctiveness of tasks doesn't mean that the content of the distinctiveness always has to be the same, but that the distinctiveness has to be maintained. If there's no longer any distinction between, let's say, doing literary study and doing historical work, then there is no longer any literary study, merely the expansion (and, I suppose, the takeover) of what was formerly literary studies by historical work. Now, I can see why *some* people—i.e., historians—might like that to happen, but I can't see why literary critics would like that to happen, unless they want to put themselves all out of a job (which sometimes they seem to want to do, curious people that they are).

Olson: You conclude *Professional Correctness* by suggesting that the best way to convince the public of the value of academic work is to hire professional lobbyists and public relations experts.

Fish: That usually gets people teed off.

Olson: Now that you are dean, have you considered doing so for your college?

Fish: No, actually. What we're doing for the college is trying to generate publicity at such a rapid rate that we in effect make *Lingua Franca,* the *Chronicle of Higher Education,* the *Chicago Tribune*, and other important media venues our publicity agents, and we've been doing that for the last year and a half. The University of Illinois at Chicago has gotten more press attention in the last couple of years than it has ever gotten before, and it actually now gets more press attention than the University of Chicago and Northwestern, partly because we're always stealing people. We just did that last week when we hired Sander Gilman. We also hired Jerry Graff. And Paul Griffiths has just come here as head of Catholic Studies.

Olson: You once predicted that by the year 2000 the traditional English department would be a "thing of the past, a museum piece," that it would likely evolve into what might be called a "department of rhetoric," with *rhetoric* being defined broadly. What are your thoughts now about the future of the English department as a department?

Fish: Let me say first of all that in relation to *that* prediction I was wrong. That's the simplest way to put it. I was just flat out wrong, and I should have known better. The conservatism of intellectual and academic institutions is more powerful than the imagination of those who predict their evolution. So here we are, and a lot of departments—I assume still the very large majority of them—are organized in traditional ways and are looking for people who teach traditional topics. And some of them are still fighting—and this is really bizarre—the old battles between theory and literature, between high art and popular culture, and all the rest. It's quite amazing to me, but some of them are still doing that. And if we get George Bush and Dick Cheney in the White House, we'll get Lynne Cheney back, and then it will start all over again. In fact, the fact that Dick Cheney is married to Lynne Cheney is a reason for anyone connected with education or humanities councils in any city in this country to vote Democratic. But I don't know whether that's going to happen.

Olson: In your ongoing crusade to demonstrate the bankruptcy of general principle, you say that academic freedom is "a bad idea, a dubious principle" because it asks us to inhabit our moral convictions loosely and to "be ready to withdraw from them whenever pursuing them would impinge on the activities and choices of others." But doesn't the liberal notion of academic freedom create the very kind of "marketplace of ideas" that some suggest is how ideas win or lose favor in the first place?

Fish: The marketplace of ideas recommended in that tradition is one that imagines the competition in effect going on behind the scenes and decided by no one. That is, if you ever ask anyone who puts the "marketplace of ideas" idea forward, "Okay, how does it work?" the only answer you'll get is the kind of answer given by Milton at one point in the *Areopagitica:* when truth and falsehood come into the plain together, if you give truth a place in the field, she will always prevail. And that's about it. As I've often said, the only argument against that is all of recorded history. I don't think that the "contestatory model" of the way ideas win out or the way movements grow and dislodge others is really what is in the mind of those who promote the marketplace of ideas. They don't have *anything* in their mind; they're just invoking a phrase.

That's why I became interested in the Holocaust denial question, because it focuses the academic freedom question. If you look at academic freedom ideology as it's often invoked, it would seem to argue strongly for the necessity of giving Holocaust deniers—especially those with academic credentials, and there are plenty of them—their fair hearing. In one paper that I wrote recently, I go back to the 1915 statement of the AAUP where the term "academic freedom" first emerged as a rallying cry. If you look at that statement, which is about ten pages long, it becomes very clear that it's not a philosophical document at all. There's nothing about "the search for truth" or "the disinterested observer" or "the marketplace of ideas"; it's all about protecting the autonomy of the guild from trustees and about acknowledging that while we used to have to protect the guild from ecclesiastical establishments, now (in 1915) this power seems to have weakened and we have a new adversary. It's clear that for them "academic freedom" means the freedom of academics to order their own business and to weed out their own incompetents—actually, there's a list: people who are incompetent, superficial, intemperate, etc. *That* notion of academic freedom by no means suggests that everyone must be given his or her chance to have a fair hearing. It means quite the reverse: that we're only going to listen to those people who meet *our* standards—that is, the standards that have emerged in the course of the history of our discipline—and the freedom is *our* freedom from external agents who would want to take this job over from us.

I like *that* idea of academic freedom very much, the original one that emerged in 1915, because it has very little to do with large, philosophical, and abstract questions and a lot to do with a very simple question: what are the conditions of our work as we conceive and desire them to be, and what institutional and political arrangements will be best suited to bring those conditions about? That, for me, is the academic freedom context.

Olson: I think what frustrates many of your readers is your typical rhetorical maneuver of first demonstrating how a certain principle or law or theory or assumption does not hold up to a certain kind of analysis, and then announcing that your analysis should not be construed as an argument for, as you say, "abandoning or even revising" it. You comment, for example, that you could "make a plausible case for retaining every feature of current First Amendment jurisprudence even though, indeed *because*, its foundations have been shown to be built on sand." What would you say is the purpose or aim of such analysis? Besides, say, delighting readers with your wit, what specifically do you hope to accomplish?

Fish: Not much, because as I say again and again in *The Trouble with Principle* and even more clearly in a piece that was published somewhat later (it was a reply to a critic in the *American Political Science Review*, and actually it's the clearest statement I've ever written on this particular issue), I am not in the business of producing outcomes. As I say at the end of "Theory Minimalism," if after having read me or heard me you go away with something useful, I will have failed, because that would mean that I'm claiming that my argument is generative of an agenda, and that's precisely what my argument *isn't*. My argument is that theoretical claims made, let's say, by foundationalists, or anti-theoretical claims made by anti-foundationalists, cannot be cashed in—that these arguments, whether you are persuaded by them or unpersuaded by them, will not alter your behavior when you're not in the arena where these arguments are made. That's what I say. I also then have to say that making that argument cannot be said to produce a certain effect or to move you in a certain direction, because if I were to make *that* claim, I would just be falling into the trap that I have accused others of falling into.

There's a certain amount of frustration that might attend the reading or hearing of such arguments because people will then say, "But what's the point? What good is it?" My reply is that if I gave you an answer to that question, I would in fact be betraying the very argument that I am making. So the next question is, "Well, why make it at all if it doesn't go anywhere and if you don't want it to go anywhere?" The answer to *that* is a very institutional, professional one: I make it because other people are making the reverse arguments, and they're wrong. I'm just pointing out that they're wrong. If I'm right, then a lot of people are wrong. Habermas is wrong. Anyone who reads and appreciates Habermas is wrong. My favorite sentence in *The*

Trouble with Principle goes something like, "As far as I am concerned, any positive reference to Habermas in the course of an argument is enough to invalidate it." Now, you have to realize, as I'm sure you do, that there are a lot of people around here these days who are invoking Habermas and the "ideal speech situation" and the "public forum" and the "orientation toward understanding" and all of that. It's all nonsense. It's totally empty nonsense. But there are a lot of people in that line of work. Of course, most of the people who would read Habermas and quote him approvingly are on the intellectual left, but they're just making the same kind of mistake as the people they attack who are speaking out for traditional values or an immutable canon or whatever it might be. So from my point of view, there are a lot of people out there making mistakes, and I'm just going to tell them that they're making mistakes. The mistakes are so deeply ingrained in the very forms of their own thought, however, that I'm in no danger of being persuasive, and I'm therefore in no danger of running out of occasions on which to make this limited—as I call it in a new essay, "parsimonious"— argument. Now that's quite a nice situation.

Olson: Throughout much of your work, you demonstrate that we all operate not from the general—the theoretical, the principled—but from the particular, the contingent, what at one point you call, borrowing the term from Charles Taylor, "inspired adhoccery." For those who worry about such things, would you discuss how adhoccery is different from relativism—you know, the "bad *R*"?

Fish: I've been arguing against relativism or arguing against a certain understanding of relativism since the 1970s, but people *still* call me a relativist. Relativism, as I have often said, is a philosophical position that one could discuss in relation to or opposition to other philosophical positions, but it's not a form of behavior that anyone could instantiate or perform because it would require that you hold your own views in an indifferent mix with the views of others and have no special commitment to them. Indeed, that is what some people on the classical liberal (with a big *L*) side recommend. For instance, Tom Nagel, whom I quote extensively in *The Trouble with Principle*, says that what you have to do (and Rawls is in the same line of work) is to regard your own views, commitments, and senses of truth, as just anyone's. Now, that seems to me (a) to be an injunction to relativism, and (b) to be impossible as a performance.

People confuse relativism with the statement that there is no overarching or neutral or transcendent perspective from the vantage point of which disputes between well-informed antagonists can be settled. That turns out in the minds of many people to be relativism, but it's *not* relativism, because it doesn't say that there are *no* truths or *no* facts of the matter. I firmly believe that there *are* truths and facts of the matter. It says, rather, that there are no mechanisms available for certainly or absolutely settling disputes between persons equally credentialed who have opposing senses of the truth or the facts of the matter. These are two *different* assertions, but people mix them up and also say that they must be in tension with each other; that is, you can't simultaneously, I am told, say, "I believe this to be absolutely true, not just true for me or true because of my education or background," and also say, "I acknowledge that the absolute truth of this may not be able to be demonstrated in ways that would be immediately accepted by all rational beings." One is an assertion of what is the truth. The other is an assertion about our common epistemological condition. They are in no way in tension with one another, but very few people, I have found, can get around to the point where they can understand that, and they think it's relativism. But it's not relativism.

Olson: You make a distinction between what you call "boutique multiculturalism" and "strong multiculturalism." The former is a "superficial or cosmetic" relation to the culture of the Other, while the latter is an "active fostering of the unique distinctiveness of particular cultures." You claim that strong multiculturalism, what Charles Taylor calls "the politics of difference," is just as unable to come to terms with difference as is boutique multiculturalism. Would you explain why?

Fish: Strong multiculturalism stays the course longer. "Boutique multiculturalism" is the multiculturalism of someone who wants to be able to say that he or she appreciates rap music or Vietnamese food or movies from Eastern Europe; this is a multiculturalism that is firmly based on the conviction that the ability to appreciate difference is underwritten by common, shared cognitive processes and moral values that everyone participates in. So there's a universalism very slightly below the surface of what I call boutique multiculturalism. "Strong multiculturalism," rather than merely appreciating different cultures, has an investment in creating conditions in which many, many cultures flourish. As I put it in that piece, it's like an endangered species act, except that the endangered species are cultures and you don't want to let any one of them die. So you appreciate the culture not simply because you can train your palate or your sensibility to enjoy its food or its music but because you have an investment of a moral kind in the pluralism of cultures. Then the question to the strong multiculturalist is, "How deep does that investment go?" And *I'm* saying that at a certain point most strong multiculturalists, when they find at the heart of the culture that they wish to allow to flourish an action or a moral attitude that they themselves cannot abide, will stop being strong multiculturalists somewhat later than a boutique multiculturalist will stop being a multiculturalist. But they will still stop being strong multiculturalists, and they will say, "*Of course* we cannot condone clitorectomy or a fatwa against Salman Rushdie or not allowing women outside unless they are entirely swathed in veils! *Of course* we can't allow that!" There will always be a moment when the so-called multiculturalist will reveal him or herself not to be one.

This argument is exactly parallel to—in fact, it is the same argument as—my free speech argument. I usually begin by pointing to Milton's *Areopagitica*, the great oration in favor of freedom of expression and an explanation of its benefits. Three-quarters of the way through, Milton says, "But, of course, I don't mean Catholics; them we extirpate." *Extirpate*, or course, means "pull out by the roots." Everybody has what I call that "substantive kicker" up his or her sleeve in relation to the First Amendment: "Well, I didn't mean *that*. No it couldn't mean *that*." And the same is true with multiculturalists: "Well, of course, we can't approve *that* part of the culture." And often that part of the culture will be the part of the culture that its internal members are dying for and in some cases killing other people for.

So *that's* the argument. That argument is very easy to make because it's so clear that multiculturalism is, as I put it, not a coherent notion. As a demographic fact, it is of course very coherent. It's here in this university in spades, as it is in other places—different cultures, different traditions, clashing value systems. It presents an administrative problem: how do we deal with pluralism? But that's quite a different thing from making a religion out of it.

Olson: In "How the Right Hijacked the Magic Words," you say that conservatives have appropriated such liberal-hallowed terms as "equal opportunity," "color-blindness," and "individual rights," repackaging them so as to use them *against* the very causes they once served. You end this short piece by saying, "so long as they are allowed to get away with it," the right wing will continue this practice and succeed in overturning a host of liberal accomplishments. How can we prevent this from happening? How do you suggest we *not* allow them to get away with it?

Fish: One thing that you can't do at this stage is to fight in order to reclaim the territory. That is, I can make those arguments, and so can others. I can explain how color-blindness is used now and why its use, for example, in Proposition 209 in California simply masks a device for making sure that certain discriminatory practices continue and can't be the basis of civil courses of action. I can also show—and this is not a hard thing to do if you are a member of the legal community—how neutrality (or, as we call it in the legal world, "facial neutrality") is often a device designed to protect the status quo. You can make all those arguments, and I've been making arguments like them for a long time, but the trouble with those arguments is that they *don't take* politically. First of all, it takes a long time to make them. It doesn't take any time for someone to say, "I'm for color-blindness," or "I'm for fairness." But then when you have to unpack "color-blindness" or "unfairness" or "merit" and show that these terms are not as simple as they appear to be and that they in fact can be invoked in ways that mask whole sets of activities that you might want to alter, that takes a long time, and people's eyes glaze over—unless you're at some kind of rally of, let's say, critical race theorists. Then it will work because every-body in the room is already primed to give the same kind of talk that you happen to be up there giving.

So what do you do? Well, I say turn away from that vocabulary completely and instead ask different sets of questions. I recommend empirical questions: What's working? What's not working? What's going to happen if we allow these practices to continue? What's going to happen if certain changes aren't made? Do we want these things to happen? If the answer is "no," then there are certain actions we are going to have to take. What are those actions? This is quite different from, Does it correspond to the requirement for fairness? Is it truly color-blind? Is it content- or viewpoint-neutral (as if anything ever was)? Those are questions that will not serve those who wish to move ahead in general in some progressive way because the content of those terms—"individual rights," "fairness," "color-blindness"—has now been fashioned by the very agendas that progressives oppose. Again, a very simple argument. That was the first op-ed piece I did for the *Times,* and I think still the best.

Olson: In *The Trouble with Principle*, you argue that the liberal response to hate speech is either to see it as "a problem" that can be fixed through education or simply to ignore it in the spirit of the First Amendment. Much more effective, you posit, is to conceive of hate speech as "what your enemy says," because then the issue is framed much more realistically as the struggle over ways of seeing the world and ways of structuring society. Thinking of hate speech as "what your enemy says" allows us, you say, to "think in terms of strategy and ask of any proposal 'Will it retard the growth of the evil I loathe and fear?'" Would you discuss the political effectivity of such a stance? I realize the irony of asking this since you have just said that you're not looking for an outcome; nonetheless, people still will ask: What practical tactics can arise from it if we really do want to oppose hate speech?

Fish: Let me back up a bit. That part of the argument in that essay should be expanded because, if I recall, it goes by fairly quickly. It's the extreme opposite of the arguments usually made, and it's an argument that I'm beginning to make in a series of ways. I'm saying, there's no such thing as hate speech. (As I often say, I'm in the "there's no such thing as" business: "There's no such thing as hate speech," and "there's no such thing as racism.") If you could identify hate speech and racism as abstract universals, that would mean that everyone who was rational would be able to recognize and perhaps turn away from instances of them. The key sentence in that section of the essay is, "Would those we think of as hate speakers accept this as a self-description?" The answer is generally "no." They don't think they're speaking hate; they think they're speaking "the truth." We think *we're* speaking the truth. What that means is that hate speech is not the name of a general mistake; hate speech is the name of a mistake made by people who believe something that you don't believe—or, in fact, believe something that you believe to be evil and dangerous. That is what hate speech is; there's no *general* category of hate speech. Once you see that, certain conclusions follow. You give up the idea of rooting out racism as if racism were a cognitive error that you could perhaps correct either by a pill or by sitting people in a room and asking them to read John Stuart Mill or John Rawls for days and days—a kind of Evelyn Waugh scenario. It doesn't happen that way. Racism and hate speech are the names of rationalities that are abhorrent to you. Therefore, you shouldn't think that your task is somehow to reeducate these persons who have been ill-served by those who have educated them formerly. These people are not in need of your therapeutic help; they are in need, from your point of view, of being defeated. It's *that* simple. Therefore, what you should try to do is defeat them.

Let's take the Holocaust denial question because it's one that I've been working on lately. Holocaust deniers use a vocabulary of openness, free inquiry, search for the truth, academic freedom, marketplace of ideas, all the evidence is never completely in, and the search must always be kept open. They use it very well. (Actually, so do creationists; it's extremely interesting.) That's their stock in trade. If you accept that vocabulary and contest it in conversations with them, they can't lose, and you've already lost, because you're playing the game on what has now become their terms. What you have to do is realize that you're not going to *persuade* Holocaust deniers to your position. You're not going to enliven or make more healthy the conversation by letting them in. They're just going to pollute the conversation. That's what they're there for. That's their job. So what you've got to do is keep them out. How do you keep them out? You keep them out in the same way that they accuse others of keeping them out: by exercising the authority that you or your colleagues have as, let's say, members of a department or a university or a press.

Remember David Irving, the Holocaust denier who lately lost a libel case that he brought against Deborah Lipstadt? One of the things that had happened to him is that a book of his scheduled to be published by St. Martin's Press was withdrawn by the press because of protests from various groups who believed, correctly, that he's in the business of Holocaust denial. When this news broke, all kinds of laments were made about academic freedom and violations of the First Amendment. That's nonsense! That was an instance of academic freedom and the First Amendment working just fine. It's not that the *government* violated his freedom. Remember what the First Amendment says: "Congress shall pass no law. . . ." It doesn't say, "St. Martin's Press shall reject no book. . . ." It doesn't say, "St. Martin's Press shall reject no book because it judges that political pressures against its publication might be injurious to its reputation." That's what St. Martin's Press is *supposed* to do! I don't know what happened in their councils, but I imagine they were sitting around and saying, "If we publish this book, we might lose the following authors who have already told us that they will not give us their next book if we publish this one. And if you look at these authors, they have been responsible for thirty-five percent of our profits last year. Let's not publish this book."

Now, that's an instance of the kind of pressure you *can* exert so as to exclude from respectable venues the works and writings of the people you oppose. In fact, in today's *Chicago Tribune* there's a piece on Joe Lieberman (in which I'm quoted extensively, by the way) on this same question. I was called by the *Tribune* the other day about

Lieberman's position against television violence, and Tipper Gore's position some years ago against rock lyrics. I said, "It sounds good to me!" It's not that I necessarily agree with the stance that Lieberman takes because I don't know it in detail, or with Tipper Gore's stance, but the idea that a public official would stand up and say something that might chill some activity of expression seems to me to be exactly right. The *wrong* thing would be—and it would be immediately declared unconstitutional—if there were some law that said that David Irving's books couldn't be published or that Quentin Tarantino's movies couldn't be made. *That,* of course, is exactly what the First Amendment says you *can't* do: "Congress shall pass no law. . . ." But acting in such a way as to stifle, suppress, embarrass, and stigmatize those whose words and writings you think to be dangerous is, I think, a perfectly good and all-American activity.

Olson: In *Excitable Speech,* Judith Butler takes a strong stand against attempts to regulate hate speech, claiming that in a very real way *the state produces hate speech:* "'Hate speech' is not deemed hateful or discriminatory until the courts decide that it is. There is no hate speech in the full sense of that term until and unless there is a court that decides that there is." Do you agree with this characterization? It sounds very much like your contention that hate speech does not exist.

Fish: What Judith is doing is making a philosophical point. She's saying that as a legal category hate speech is only born, as it were, when there is a law against it, so it is in that way produced by acts of the state. I think that is correct in the context of her analysis, but there's another sense in which hate speech is a name that has been identified by those against whom it is directed, and then they try to get laws in place to penalize using such language. I'm not sure where Judith's argument goes. In other words, I'd be willing to say that I think that she is correct in her description, and then I would ask, "And therefore what?" Usually, at least in this context, I then would get off of her train for the reasons that I give quite fully in the chapter where I consider her work.

If you remember that argument, I'm saying that Judith believes or says she believes that certain forms of hate speech or what are called hate speech against blacks, gays, Jews, women, or whomever it might be should not be penalized or criminalized because they allow opportunities for creative rejoinders of the kind most famously noted in the sixties when the "Black is Beautiful" slogan became powerful, or when gay activists shouted, "We're here, we're queer, get used to it," and so forth. Those are instances in which, as Judith puts it, the supposed invective is appropriated by its target and held up either as a banner or as a weapon that can be sent back in the direction of those who hurled it in the first place. I think, again, that this is a description of what happens, but it seems to me that to make that into a general principle of law is a mistake because it ignores the specificity of particular verbal acts that some might feel wounded by. Indeed, that's a specificity that, as you know from my analysis, Judith herself later subscribes to when she tries to make a case for allowing pornography and other forms of *sexually* directed speech that some find troublesome, but then wants to have regulations against *racist* speech. Of course, given her general argument she shouldn't be able to make that distinction or should have no motivated, principled (if you'll pardon the word) basis for making it, which leads me to say that the good thing about her position is that she doesn't believe in it when it comes down to the nitty-gritty. But she's a very smart person.

Olson: As you've just said, part of your argument about the liberal response to hate speech is to demonstrate that in effect "there is no such thing as hate speech, if you mean by that designation speech that would be judged hateful by an *independent* norm." That is, what is hateful to one may not be to another. Now, you've already said that there are ways to counteract such speech, as in the example of St. Martin's Press, and so on. As someone intensely interested in the judicial system, do you believe there is *any* general legal remedy to harmful speech or to, say, pornography?

Fish: There are places in which the law recognizes—or, as Judith would say, by recognizing brings into being—a category of speech subject to judicial regulation. For example, there are in many states penalty enhancement laws—that is, laws that add to a sentence for an act of, let's say, assault or robbery, an additional penalty in terms usually of a sentence or perhaps a fine if it can be shown that the crime has been motivated by racial or gender bias. This has been declared constitutional by the Supreme Court in the Mitchell case. There are other areas in which that argument or forms of that argument have not been successful, notably in the speech code cases with the University of Wisconsin, the University of Michigan, and Stanford University (these, I think, are the three most important cases). The court—I think largely influenced by the image of the university as the place where the freest exchange or ideas is a mandate and an obligation—has wanted to give university contexts the largest latitude and has rejected the offensiveness argument. So I think that you have to make distinctions, as the law itself does.

That's one of the very good things about the essay by Robert Post that I talk about in one of my chapters, and also the essay by Frederick Schauer of Harvard's Kennedy School of Government. They point out in their own different ways (and I agree with them) that there is no general judicial doctrine of free expression; there are a bunch of them in relation to the contextual, situational settings in which these questions emerge. Strong or pure free speech theorists always want to start not with context-particular settings and the problems of expression that then arise from them, but with some general overview of speech, and then the context is supposed to be somehow adjudicated in relation to that general, overriding sense of speech. But as Schauer and Post and others have said, and I agree, there is no such general context. So, in connection with this topic the law will make its way in what might be called by an outside observer a somewhat contingent and revisable manner.

Olson: Conceiving hate speech and other such issues as a struggle between adversaries over opposing ways of seeing the world is reminiscent of Ernesto Laclau and Chantal Mouffe's notion of hegemonic struggle. Do you find their work useful in thinking about your own understanding of politics?

Fish: Not much. The only writing that I've done in any detailed way is in an article in which I talk about an essay by Chantal Mouffe. It seems to me that Chantal, along with other people, is making a double argument, and one that I think turns on itself. She's arguing, on the one hand, correctly, that normative liberal theorists in the Rawls tradition or in the Kant-through-Rawls tradition make the mistake of thinking that politics can be quarantined or eliminated, and then she and others on the left just make the mistake in a slightly more rarified way. They think that politics can be managed. What I keep saying to all of them is that there is nothing general to say about politics at all. There is, of course, a lot to do *within* it, but there's nothing general to say *about* it. And I find that they are still in the looking-for-something-general-to-say-about-it business.

Olson: So, you don't find the notion of hegemonic struggle to be useful.

Fish: No. It would not be comfortable for me to speak in those Frankfurt School accents. It's just not a tradition of thought that I've ever found useful.

Olson: It is not uncommon to hear colleagues say that you "revolution-ized" our understanding of reading/interpretation, or that you are the "most influential" scholar of English studies in the last quarter of a century or even the last half of a century. Of course, in the last several decades English studies has been influenced by a range of other discourses, such as deconstruction, postcolonial theory, and cultural studies. How would you describe your legacy, your contribution to English studies?

Fish: Well, I think that the essays and books on Milton, Herbert, Donne, Marvell, Jonson, Burton, and Bacon are still doing work in their fields—that is, in the communities that I addressed when I wrote them. And I think that for a while at least (who can put a date on it?) that interpretive work will still be found either helpful or an obstacle to understanding; therefore we must engage it. Now, I'm not sure about the other work, the work on legal theory or First Amendment theory or general interpretive theory or pragmatist theory or reader response theory—I'm not sure. I think that the advantage I might have over some others who address the same questions is the accessibility of my writing, that people do not feel when they read my work that they are required to learn an entirely new vocabulary or have a special dictio-nary made up. That means that you can assign it to students, who may not find it easy going in some ways but who will not find it full of technical terms that prove to be obstacles to them. So in that sense I think that the style of the writing might give it a chance to be around for a while.

Another thing that can happen to you (you cannot engineer this) is that you can be put "on the list," as I like to put it. By "the list" I mean that everybody writes shorthand accounts of this and that: "cite three or four names that stand for *X*." If you get onto that list, that means that you're going to be around for a little while. So, I may be around if I'm on the list, as I sometimes am with Rorty, Kuhn, Derrida, or whomever. A couple weeks ago, Jim Atlas wrote a piece about Al Gore's reading habits in which he wonders why Gore doesn't read Derrida and me. I think there are very good answers to that question, but, you see, what I'm saying is that the *name* and therefore to some extent the *work* achieves a certain currency that is entirely an accident of rolodexes. (I happen to know Jim Atlas, but that's irrelevant to the point.) When people are searching for a few names to put on the list that would be identified either as, let's say, "cutting-edge," or as "enemies of civili-zation," then I—not always, but sometimes—will be one of those names. But I didn't do that. That's just the fact that there were some newspaper and magazine pieces twelve or thirteen years ago, and then the set of names to which you might refer in shorthand to make a point is solidified by journalists—and there I am. It's bizarre in a lot of ways because usually I'm there in ways that are totally inaccurate: Fish the relativist. Actually, the best that I've seen recently (and I wrote a little bit about this) was in *Heterodoxy*, which is David Horowitz's journal. There was a piece in it—it must have been in January or February, 2000—in which I am referred to as a Communist! I thought, this is really something! As a Communist! So it's that kind of thing—where your name becomes something that people can just plop into a sentence and put next to a noun or an adjective without any strong sense of what any of the writing is like.

Olson: But certainly if you look at any of the anthologies of the great critical statements, the introductions will always say that your early reader-response work completely changed how professors and students of literature read literature.

Fish: Well, the legacy of reader response is, I think, pedagogical. That is, what it does and what it did do is allow students into the conversation in a classroom. If you get the idea that students who read are performing certain kinds of both cognitive and emotional acts as they read and you can get them to reflect on them in a way that is analytic rather than exclusively personally revelatory, you have a method of teaching that to some extent lessens the distance between students and the works they sometimes fear. That is, it diminishes to a certain extent the alienation factor. So that I think is one good pedagogical legacy of reader-response. Otherwise, I think of reader-response criticism as a stage in the movement away from formalism, but introduced not actually historically before poststructuralism but before poststructuralism became well discussed in the United States.

Olson: I have always argued that if it weren't for reader response, we wouldn't have accepted deconstruction as early as we did.

Fish: Well, it's possible that that's true. If you'll remember, there are at least four important people outside of the United States who were also doing reader-oriented work: there were Jauss and Iser in Germany; there was Roland Barthes, especially in *S/Z;* and there was Riffaterre, who actually was in this country, although he's very French. And earlier than any of us, in the late thirties, there was Louise Rosenblatt. I think it was 1938 when she published her big book. So this often happens: people are working in slightly different ways in the same direction. There's also at the same time the work coming out of classes taught by Reuben Brower at Harvard University, which produced books like Norman Rabkin's *Shakespeare and the Common Understanding*, Paul Alpers' *The Poetry of the Faerie Queene*, and Stephen Booth's book on Shakespeare's *Sonnets*—all pretty much coming out at the same time. There was also the revival of strong interest in rhetoric, sponsored to some extent by the work of Chaim Perelman, but also in a more accessible way for most literary scholars here by Wayne Booth and others. And that all happened, you'll remember, within a ten-year period, so there were a lot of influences. And then, of course, there was Norman Holland's and David Bleich's psychoanalytic work. Well, people can read all about this in Jane's anthology.

Olson: This is the last question, and you've actually anticipated it, as you often do. It is traditional to end an interview by asking if there are any criticisms or misunderstandings of your work that you'd like to take issue with at this time.

Fish: Well, they're all related. There are people who think I'm a relativist, and I've already spoken to why that is in fact false. There are people who think I glorify subjectivity, where in fact if there's a criticism to be made of my work, it's that it doesn't leave any room for subjectivity or for independent choice because of its emphasis on interpretive communities, or on the way in which disciplines work, or the requirements of positions within an institution's structure, like the judiciary or university administration. So that's obviously a mistake that is continually made, and it seems to me to be a mistake that indicates that the reader didn't get past the first page, if he or she even got to the first page. So I don't know what I could do about that. The third error or mistake that I find often made is thinking that because I will not draw any conclusions from my anti-theoretical argument or from my anti-anti-theoretical argument, the conclusion drawn for me is that I'm a quietist, or that I'm urging persons to tend their own gardens. I'm just saying that if you're looking for ways in which to underwrite your activism—whether it's institutional activism or activism in the city or state—then you're not going to find it in these large abstractions, and you're not going to find it in an argument like mine against these large abstractions. You're going to find it in whatever urgencies and imperatives seem compelling to you in the empirical context that led you to be a political worker in the first place. But people don't see that and they think that I'm arguing for quietism.

Those would be the mistakes or mischaracterizations of my work that most often appear, and they seem ineradicable as far as I can tell. They keep turning up over and over again, and what always amazes me, especially when I give a talk or participate in a panel, is that the people in the audience raise these questions, and you can tell from the tone of their voice that they do so in the firm conviction that I have never heard them before. That is the amazing thing. "Oh really?" As with anyone who has been in any other professional practice for some time, I've been at this for a while, so I've heard these questions before. But the people who for whatever reasons are discomfited by these arguments really strongly believe (a) that they have thought up the knock-down response, and (b) that I never would have heard it before. That's almost, how shall I say, . . . cute.

Afterword

J. Hillis Miller

I am not quite sure what I'm doing here, at the tail end of this quite remarkable book. I feel a little like a dissonant voice in the midst of a dialogue of one, or an interruption in a harmonious duet. *Justifying Belief* might, however, be thought of as solo with piano accompaniment, with me as the stage hand who noisily drops something just at the moment the performance is over. Or I might be thought of as the awkward clown who comes on stage to interrupt a graceful pas de deux.

Surely *Justifying Belief* is the best introduction to Stanley Fish's work yet written. It is a marvel of clarity and accuracy. Gary Olson has an amazing ability to speak for Fish. He adopts Fish's own style in an eerie species of ventriloquism. As is always the case with indirect discourse, however, a certain degree of irony enters into Olson's acts of 'speaking for' Fish. I would not quite say that if you read *Justifying Belief* you do not need to read Fish. For those in a hurry, however, it is the next best thing. Of course, lots of Fish himself is cited verbatim in this book, especially in the interviews that make up the last two chapters.

My credentials for commenting on *Justifying Belief* or on Stanley Fish's work are slender. I have not, so far as I know, been all that deeply influenced by his work. I greatly admire it, however. The evidence for that, such as it is, is that I have twice made serious attempts (both unsuccessful) to get Fish as a colleague. I even participated in the invitation to him to come as a visitor to Johns Hopkins. He came in a year

141

when I was on leave. That visit led to Fish's move to Hopkins, but after I had left. So I have never had the pleasure of attending department meetings with him. It must be an interesting experience. Perhaps my first encounter with Fish in action, certainly the first I remember, was an impressive performance at the School of Criticism and Theory in 1979, when it was still at Irvine. It was not so much the lecture itself that I remember, but rather his handling of the discussion period afterward. He responded to not very promising questions with immense wit and rhetorical force. He paced back and forth on the auditorium stage and improvised brilliantly for more than an hour. At the end he was still as fresh as ever. He cheerfully offered to continue the discussion with any and all at his office hours the next day. I also remember vividly a private discussion with Fish at a colleague's house at Yale. I tried, unsuccessfully, to persuade him that the words of a text constrain to some degree the meanings that an "interpretative community" can project into it. No, he insisted, the text is a complete blank, without any force of its own to limit what we may make it mean. He needed, of course, to hold to that counterintuitive position in order to sustain his general project.

The carrying out of that project has made Stanley Fish without doubt the most clear-headed and logical explorer of the consequences of an anti-foundational position. He has been remorselessly consistent in attacking those on the left or on the right who try in one way or another to wiggle out of the consequences of a strict anti-foundationalism. Examples, abundantly demonstrated in Olson's scrupulous reading of Fish's positions, are his disdain for the notion that theory has practical use, his refusal of appeals to principle, his argument that there is no such thing as hate speech or freedom of speech, his scorn for liberalism, and his claim that neither theory nor appeal to principle nor academic literary study nor cultural studies nor academic multiculturalism, valuable enterprises though they may be, has any consequences, especially not the sort of consequences—political amelioration or making the world better—for which their practitioners hope. Nor, Fish repeatedly asserts, will his own work have consequences. If it does, he says, it will have failed.

In place of all these appeals to some foundation or other, Fish puts the claim that spontaneous and unreasoned belief, what is "heartfelt," actually governs behavior. This is accompanied by what he calls localism or an appeal to specific situations. In each situation, adhoccery (a wonderful word!), rules of thumb, mastery of rhetorical devices, should determine what will work to accomplish what you want to accomplish. It is impossible to get outside some situation or other and see things from an objective or disinterested perspective. It's a good thing too. It is wrong, for example, according to Fish, to say that free speech ought to mean giving those who deny the Holocaust a chance to speak. If you believe that such people are wrong and dangerous, you should consider them your enemies and do everything you can to deny them a hearing. The human situation, for Fish, is agonistic through and through. We need to face that, and to fight for our lives—or, what is the same thing, to fight for our beliefs, even though they have no justification whatsoever in solid foundational principles of any sort, even the foundation of a concept of situationalism. They are just the beliefs we happen to have.

It is a risky business to try to disagree with Fish. This is true not only because he is a powerful, indefatigable, and joyful polemicist whose arguments are logically airtight, but also because he has usually foreseen objections and has given them a lethal counterpunch before you have even thought to raise them. Nevertheless, I shall dare to make a couple of points, partly directed to Olson's account, partly to Fish's own work.

Though Olson mentions more than once Fish's justifiable pride in his work on Milton and other seventeenth-century authors, I think more might have been made of this part of Fish's work. I say this not because it contradicts anything Olson says, but because Fish is a brilliant reader of literary works. I think not only, for example, of all the work on Milton—for instance, Fish's deep understanding of Milton's prose work—but of a wonderful essay of 1975 on *Coriolanus* that has always stuck in my mind: "Speech-Act Theory, Literary Criticism, and *Coriolanus*." Something might have been said about Fish's procedures as a literary critic and literary scholar. These are exemplary. Fish makes much of his commitment to the craft of writing. Those within the discipline of English studies could learn much by attending to how he practices that craft when he is doing a reading.

Remembering the *Coriolanus* essay will allow me to make two further points. Fish's brilliant readings are characteristically not just readings but also works of—I don't know any other way to put it—theory. Even if it is a theory against theory, the *Coriolanus* essay is about speech-act theory and is theoretical itself. Were Fish *not* a theorist, his work would not have received so much attention. It is, consequently, a little disingenuous of him to attack theory, since doing so is biting the hand that feeds him.

My second point is that Olson does not perhaps make enough, nor perhaps even does Fish himself, of the relation of his work to speech-act theory. In the 1991 interview, Fish affirms that J.L. Austin has been one of his stylistic models, but he does not say that he has been greatly influenced by what Austin has to say with such stylistic flair in *How to Do Things With Words*. Perhaps he hasn't. Nevertheless, one of the weaknesses of Fish's arguments, or at any rate of Olson's account of them, is that they are presented as purely logical rather than as also to a degree performative. Fish is quite right to say that a purely logical argument or an airtight series of constative statements has no necessary consequences. You do not persuade someone to stop being in love by pointing out that the person's beloved has a double chin, a nasty temper, or some other defect. You don't argue a racist out of racism by saying that racism is inhumane. The racist thinks his or her views are the truth. Nevertheless, Fish thinks of himself as a rhetorician as well as a logician. Rhetoric, however, is performative as well as a way to make forceful logical or constative arguments.

A good definition of *rhetoric* is to say that it is the use of words to make something happen. The subtitle of Olson's book is *Stanley Fish and the Work of Rhetoric*. Paradoxically, in spite of Fish's attention to rhetoric, he could be defined as primarily a brilliant practitioner of logical argument. He is someone who subordinates rhetoric to logic, someone who uses grammar and rhetoric in the service of logic. (I allude, of course, to the three domains of the medieval trivium.) Fish's writings, nevertheless, have a powerful performative component, even though in saying his work should have no consequences he wants to deny that it does. Fish's writings are a way of doing things with words. It is misleading of him to say that his work will have failed unless it has no consequences. What he writes is not a neutral logical argument but, in part at least, a speech act designed to influence belief and action. To say, "I don't expect to change people and will have failed if I do so," as Fish repeatedly does, is a transparent rhetorical ploy designed to make his argument more performatively effective. It is like saying, "I don't expect to make you fall out of love by telling you that your beloved is ugly, but I cannot hide the truth: you have a mistaken view of your beloved."

Insofar as what Fish writes is a performative use of language, it will have consequences, though perhaps not the ones he foresees or intends. Surely that has been the case. Fish's work, for example, has at least had the effect of arousing the ire of many readers on the left and on the right. It may have made them more obdurate in holding what he views as mistaken opinions. It has also had the effect of giving Fish the pleasure of feeling that he is right while almost everyone else is wrong. His writings have *generated* that pleasure, which is probably one of the chief reasons he writes so tirelessly, essay after essay. As he says, believing that you are right and knowing that an inexhaustible supply of incorrigibly wrong-headed thinkers exists is "quite a nice situation." Further investigation of the relation of Fish's rhetorical theory and practice to speech-act theory and practice would usefully extend Olson's account.

A key word in Fish's putdown of appeals to theory or principle is "belief." Fish says in the 1991 interview that he has made frequent use in his teaching of the verse from Hebrews: "Now faith is the substance of things hoped for, the evidence of things unseen." He might also have cited what the risen Jesus says to Thomas Didymus ("Doubting Thomas") in John 20: 29: "Thomas, because thou hast seen me, thou hast believed: blessed are they that have not seen, and yet have believed." Fish's concept of belief is discussed a good bit by Olson in a subsection of Chapter 3 entitled "Rhetoric and the Justification of Belief." For Fish, belief, as it exists in a given person, seems to be more or less taken for granted as something irrational, spontaneous, and not amenable to correction by argument. As such, belief is not "justifiable" by logical argument. We just believe what we believe. Belief could be defined as the foundational concept of Fish's anti-foundationalism. It is the rock bottom on which the edifice of his argument is erected. "In many ways," says Olson, paraphrasing Fish, "we have little control over our beliefs. No one shops for a belief and then consciously chooses one from an array of competing beliefs; rather, the act of believing is involuntary, more a matter of reflex than cogitation. Acquiring a belief is more akin to catching a cold than to selecting a new shirt."

Just what is belief? What does it mean to say, "I believe so and so," or perhaps only unselfconsciously to hold that belief without ever articulating it? That is a very big question, requiring for its answer a lengthy discussion. I suggest, however, that holding a belief is more than a little like being in love. Sooner or later, if a belief is ever to enter into the outer world and have effects there, it will need to be expressed in some language that is a version of "I believe so and so," or in some gesture or act that substitutes for that statement, just as sooner or later the lover says "I love you." Both "I love you" and "I believe so and so" are performative utterances that have the peculiarity of generating the thing they appear to name. Just as you do not fall in love until you say, "I love you," so you do not believe until you say, "I believe," or until you emit some gesture or sign that stands in for that utterance. Beliefs do not come from nowhere, nor were we born with a ready-made genetically determined structure of beliefs. We are interpellated by parents, school, church, government, and, perhaps most of all, the media to believe what we do believe. Belief is ideology. If the President says often enough that we are at war with terrorism and that terrorists are "evil," even though war has not been formally declared, and even though the word "war" must be being used figuratively, since the word literally defines armed strife between sovereign nations, people come to believe that. They then are willing to accept the suspension of constitutionally guaranteed civil liberties, "liberty and justice for all," that happens in wartime. The President's apparently constative statements have been performatively effective. If belief may be defined as ideology, like ideology it invites understanding by way of some version of speech-act theory. That analysis is missing in Olson's book, though it may exist in one of Fish's writings unknown to me.

My final point: Fish persuasively argues that the profession of English literature studies has as its goal the elucidation of meanings in texts written in English and deemed to be literature. As such, the profession of English makes sense as a discipline. It has its own internal rules, protocols, and tacit assumptions. These are taken for granted by those within the discipline as "the sort of thing we do around here." It is to a considerable degree this self-enclosure that makes it laughable, according to Fish, to think that English professors should undertake to have political impact through their professional work, however good it may be for them to be politically active outside that professional work. This self-enclosure also means that it is suicidal for those in English studies to expand their discipline in the direction of some all-embracing cultural studies. It is suicidal because it would mean that professors of English would lose their raison d'être and the specificity of their professional discipline. That discipline has never had a political justification. Trying to give it one is a big mistake.

I think Fish somewhat exaggerates the degree to which English studies has ever been unified in a shared agreement about "what we do around here." Many English professors, myself included, have always had a sense of wanting to do, and actually doing, something that does not quite fit "what we do around here." That, however, is not the main final point I want to make. Fish, as Olson reads him, makes it sound as if English professors are willfully destroying their discipline. They are doing this by a laughably mistaken desire to be politically effective and out of a bleeding-heart liberal sympathy for those who have been oppressed by patriarchy and imperialism. I do not think it is quite that simple. The old profession of English literary studies had a quite definite political role in American society. Literature, especially English literature—that is, paradoxically, the literature of a country we defeated over two hundred years ago in a war of independence—was seen as a primary repository of our country's ethos and national values. Therefore, it was a good thing to teach it. It was also a good thing to find out all the facts about English literature, even the most remote facts—let's say, for example, the facts about the early life of John Marston, not to mention the early life of John Milton. We lived in a country where what Simon During calls "literary subjectivity—characterized by a love of literature" was a widespread feature of social and individual life. To put this another way, literature was a major means of interpellating people into the reigning national ideology. English departments, therefore, had a justified place in universities and colleges.

That role for literature (and hence for English departments) is rapidly fading. It is being replaced by other media: cinema, television, popular music, computer games, the Internet. As a result, those deeply invested in the discipline of English literary studies—like me, and like Fish too— have been left high and dry, with less and less of a social function. It is not surprising that someone with Stanley Fish's desire to be effective in the world should spend more and more of his time teaching law or writing about it, or writing about hate speech and Holocaust doubters, or writing op-ed pieces on such topics for the *New York Times*. It is not surprising that there should be a turn, especially by younger people brought up on the new media, to the study of those media that do have political, ideological, and social force. These new media now more and more make American citizens what they are or lead them to believe what they do believe. Belief, as I said above, does not come out of nowhere. People are called or interpellated to believe. Shakespeare, Wordsworth, Austen, and Dickens used to do that. Now it is television, or the network news, or the latest film, song, or computer game. A fuller accounting of the social role literary study used to have and of the way literature's social role is now fading is a missing ingredient in Fish's description, as Olson reports it, of what he calls "the discipline of English studies."

I am sure my friend Stanley, if he reads this, will say (or try to prove) that my arguments are without merit. Or, more likely, he will claim that he has already foreseen all I say and has already abundantly responded to the points I make. I would then have some things to say in reply to that. The interchange is potentially without end, which is the way Stanley Fish likes it.

University of California
Irvine, California

Notes

Introduction

1. Harpham was writing in the *Times Literary Supplement* and Cunningham was writing in the *New Statesman and Society*.

2. In *There's No Such Thing as Free Speech*, Fish comments on the five debates and on who won: "I am always asked, 'Who won?' By our [Fish and D'Souza's] reckoning, which could surely be disputed, the debates ended in a draw: two each and a tie. What cannot be disputed, because it was reported to us at every turn, is that the campus communities won as they always will when important questions are taken up by serious and informed opponents" (52).

Chapter 1

Public Intellectuals and the Discipline of English Studies

1. With very few exceptions, such poets were in fact men (hence the use of the male pronoun).

2. It's fatal to the ambitions of the new historicists for obvious reasons, given Fish's argument; it is fatal to the fears of those who oppose them in that many conservative critics have openly expressed concern that if the new historicists have their way, English studies will become a branch of left-wing politics. Since in Fish's eyes the new historicists have no chance whatsoever of succeeding, both the ambitions *and* the fears are unfounded. Fish writes,

> What this means is that both the fear provoked by the new
> historicism, that it will lead to the substitution of partisan political

agendas for the decorums and standards thought proper to the academy, and the hope attached to the new historicism, that it will lead to the substitution of partisan political agendas for the decorums and standards thought proper to the academy, are jointly unrealizable; the fear because performances in the academy must take a certain obligatory form; the hope because the form academic performances take, whether it is achieved "sincerely" or as a matter of strategy, will not allow those performances to be effective outside the very special precincts of the academic world. (51–52)

3. I should make clear that Fish himself does not say that the avenues of connection between literary work and political power have been broken for "at least two centuries." He does, however, point to the strong connection between the two in the sixteenth and seventeenth centuries, and I can't believe that anyone would argue that—at least in the context of Great Britain—the Romantics or Victorians enjoyed any significant entrée to political power vis-à-vis their pens.

4. Fish anticipates the argument that perhaps we could engage in *both* activities: social-oriented criticism and close literary analysis. He writes, "One might think it would be possible to pay double attention, at one moment doing full justice to the verbal intricacy of a poem and at the next inquiring into the agendas in whose service that intricacy has been put. But here one must recall the difficulty of serving two masters; each will be jealous of the other and demand fidelity to its imperatives" (69).

5. Fish says this is a "question of the direction of force." That is, change is flowing *from* the social movements *to* the academic areas of study, not the reverse (86).

6. Fish also makes this point quite forcefully in "Critical Self-Consciousness, Or Can We Know What We're Doing?"

7. He points out that such a state is akin to the internalization of deity, and while this would be conceivable in a religious context, it would not be conceivable in the "militantly secular tradition" of cultural studies (104).

8. The "cameo" or "rent for a day" intellectual, says Fish, is the "media equivalent of an expert witness" (119).

9. Another point that Fish makes regarding this issue is that if we *all* are being urged to become public intellectuals, the field would soon be "overcrowded" with public intellectuals, leaving no one to "labour in the ever smaller vineyards of the academy" (116).

10. By "those who now occupy that role," Fish means the various commentators who actually could be called "public intellectuals" because they have easy access to national forums of communication and because they expatiate on a wide range of subjects but who, because of their right-wing orientation or lack of academic status, would *not* be called public intellectuals by the

very academics calling for the "return" of the public intellectual. Fish is referring to such figures as Dinesh D'Souza, Roger Kimball, and William Buckley.

11. Interestingly, in the interview in chapter 5, Fish claims that in his capacity as dean of the College of Liberal Arts and Sciences at the University of Illinois at Chicago, he has not hired lobbyists; however, he is quite proud of the college's ability to use the media to its advantage.

12. As I pointed out earlier, Fish first conceived the outline and thrust of these arguments for a workshop that he conducted in 1990 at the Folger Library in Washington, D.C.; however, for many people in English studies, their first exposure to these arguments was the presentation in Alabama.

13. Corkin is referring to Fish's "The Common Touch, or, One Size Fits All," published in a collection edited by Gless and Herrnstein Smith.

14. There are, of course, many compositionists who object to the introduction of cultural studies into rhetoric and composition, among them Susan Miller. Such opponents usually argue that analyzing cultural texts—television advertisements, films, music videos, other cultural forms—takes valuable classroom time away from the crucial activity of writing and analyzing students' own writing.

15. Of course, I am not suggesting that Fish is completely unaware of rhetoric and composition. He serves as an editorial board member of *JAC*, and he has at times engaged the field's scholarship. See, for example, his "Anti-Foundationalism," which I discuss in chapter 2.

Chapter 2

No Loss, No Gain: The Argument against Principle

1. Chomsky's "competence model" refers to the innate linguistic competence that all native speakers of a language are born with; thus, the rules governing the capacity to produce language are timeless and unchanging. The "performance model" accounts for language production that is affected by the specific situations of particular language makers. A speaker's sentence may not always reflect the speaker's innate linguistic competence because it has become contaminated by factors arising from the speaker's context. For Fish, however, the competence model really doesn't exist; every utterance is the product of the performance model of language use.

2. Fish is responding to an argument by Adena Rosmarin, who cites William Empson's *Seven Types of Ambiguity*, W.J. Harvey's *Character in the Novel*, and Barbara Herrnstein Smith's *Poetic Closure* as examples of the kinds of works that extend beyond specific interpretations of individual works and that might thus be thought of as theoretical.

3. Theory has had one additional effect in literary studies according to Fish: academics who engage in it can reap certain material rewards, including tenure, promotion, merit-pay increases, and job offers, but such consequences, again, are not the strong sense of consequence that proponents of theory have in mind when they tout its benefits. In an unusual moment of humor, Fish writes,

> Those who do [theory] can be published, promoted, fired, feted, celebrated, reviled; there can be symposia devoted to it, journals committed to it; there can be departments of theory, schools of theory; it can be a rallying cry ("Give me theory or give me death!"), a banner, a target, a program, an agenda. . . . But although these are certainly the consequences of theory, they are not theoretical consequences" (337).

4. For example, Fish criticizes Kenneth Bruffee's application of social constructionist thought to collaborative learning (which itself draws on Fish's work) for promulgating "a political vision that has at its center the goal of disinterestedly viewing contending partisan perspectives which are then either reconciled or subsumed in some higher or more general synthesis, in a larger and larger *consensus*." Such a goal, says Fish, is "incompatible with antifoundationalism because it assumes the possibility of getting a perspective on one's beliefs" (350).

5. Several people, Patricia Bizzell and Robert Scholes among them, have made precisely that point, according to Fish.

6. In his discussion of boutique and strong multiculturalism, Fish draws on Charles Taylor's distinction between "a politics of equal dignity" and the "politics of difference." See Taylor's "The Politics of Recognition."

7. In a private conversation, he once referred to conservatives as "a bunch of thugs" and liberals as "foolish and silly." See the interview in chapter 4.

8. By "outlaws," Fish means those considered unsuitable to engage in the rational discussion of differences—fanatics, fundamentalists, those disrespectful of others' fundamental beliefs, and the like.

9. Fish remarks in the interview in chapter 5, "As I often say, I'm in the 'there's no such thing as' business."

10. For an excellent discussion (and description) of the futility of trying to persuade someone to stop being a racist, see Spigelman.

11. Fish complicates the issue even further by stating that in response to a particular instance of hate speech you may on occasion even invoke a principle such as tolerance, in which case you would be sounding, for the moment, like a liberal; but there is nothing wrong with that strategy, says Fish, "as long as you don't take your liberalism too seriously and don't hew to it as a matter of principle" (72).

Chapter 3

The Story of Rhetoric: Constructing the Ground
Upon Which You Confidently Walk

1. Fish notes that to some (especially to natural law theorists) collapsing these two categories would be a *good* idea, if only for the sake of efficiency; however, he reminds them that since society supports many moralities there would be many and conflicting laws rather than a "single abiding standard to which disputing parties might have recourse" (142).

2. Fish refers in particular to James Boyd White, but he also cites Peter Goodrich and Clare Dalton.

3. This argument may sound familiar, in that it is in effect the premise of the Clarendon Lectures. Fish is saying that such metacritical inquiry threatens the distinctiveness of legal practice because it is a *different* endeavor with its own objectives—objectives that are *not* first and foremost the winning of the case at hand.

4. In addition to this caveat, Fish also points out that in describing "how the law works," he is not making the law into an ahistorical abstraction. If anything, his account privileges the historical by demonstrating that the law is always rhetorical, contingent, and context dependent. It is only "a philosophical parlor trick" that attempts to turn his "insistence on historicity into something ahistorical" (178).

5. Although the essay reprinted in *The Trouble with Principle* is titled "Faith Before Reason," the original was titled "A Reply to Richard Neuhaus." Neuhaus' essay was entitled "Why We Can Get Along."

6. In this discussion, Fish cites philosopher John Heil, who wrote that "acquiring a belief is equivalent to catching a cold" (283).

7. In the preceding phrase, Fish is paraphrasing Protagoras.

Works Cited

Austin, J.L. *How To Do Things with Words*. London: Oxford UP, 1962.

Corkin, Stanley. "Afterthoughts: When Is an English Teacher Not an English Teacher?" Raymond 175–77.

Dalton, Clare. "An Essay in the Deconstruction of Contract Doctrine." *Yale Law Review* 94 (1985): 997–1114.

Dobrin, Sidney I. "English Departments and the Question of Disciplinarity." *College English* 59 (1997): 692–99.

Fish, Stanley. "Anti-Foundationalism, Theory Hope, and the Teaching of Composition." *Doing* 342–55.

———. "Beliefs about Belief." *Trouble* 279–84.

———. "Boutique Multiculturalism." *Trouble* 56–72.

———. "Consequences." *Doing* 315–41.

———. "Critical Self-Consciousness, Or Can We Know What We're Doing?" *Doing* 346–67.

———. *Doing What Comes Naturally: Change, Rhetoric, and the Practice of Theory in Literary and Legal Studies*. Durham: Duke UP, 1989.

———. "Faith Before Reason." *Trouble* 263–75.

————. "The Law Wishes to Have Formal Existence." *There's No Such Thing as Free Speech and It's a Good Thing, Too.* New York: Oxford UP, 1994. 141–79.

————. *Professional Correctness: Literary Studies and Political Change.* Oxford: Clarendon, 1995.

————. "Rhetoric." *Doing* 471–502.

————. "Taking Sides." *Trouble* 1–15.

————. "Them We Burn: Violence and Conviction in the English Department." Raymond 160–73.

————. *There's No Such Thing as Free Speech and It's a Good Thing, Too.* New York: Oxford UP, 1994.

————. *The Trouble with Principle.* Cambridge: Harvard UP, 1999.

————. "Why We Can't All Just Get Along." *Trouble* 243–62.

Frus, Phyllis. "Afterthoughts." Raymond 178–80.

Goodman, Nelson. *Ways of Worldmaking.* Indianapolis: Hackett, 1978.

Goodrich, Peter. *Legal Discourse: Studies in Linguistics, Rhetoric, and Legal Analysis.* New York: St. Martin's, 1987.

Graff, Gerald. "Is There A Conversation in This Curriculum? Or, Coherence without Disciplinarity." Raymond 11–28.

Harpham, Geoffrey Galt. Introduction to "Consequences." *The Stanley Fish Reader.* Ed. H. Aram Veeser. Malden, MA: Blackwell, 1999.

Heil, John. "Belief." *A Companion to Epistemology.* Ed. Jonathan Dancy and Ernest Sosa. Cambridge: Blackwell, 1992. 45–48.

Herbert, George. "The Flower." *The Poems of George Herbert.* London: Oxford UP, 1961. 156-57.

Hobbes, Thomas. *Leviathan.* Ed. C.B. Macpherson. New York: Penguin, 1968.

Jameson, Fredric. *The Political Unconscious: Narrative as a Socially Symbolic Act.* Ithaca: Cornell UP, 1981.

Kramer, Matthew H. *Legal Theory, Political Theory, and Deconstruction: Against Rhadamanthus*. Bloomington: Indiana UP, 1991.

Kuhn, Thomas S. *The Structure of Scientific Revolutions*. Chicago: U of Chicago P, 1962.

Lauter, Paul. "Afterthoughts." Raymond 182–86.

Miller, Susan. "Technologies of Self?-Formation." *JAC* 17 (1997): 497–500.

Neuhaus, Richard. "Why We Can Get Along." *First Things* 60 (1996): 27–34.

Raymond, James C. *English As A Discipline; Or, Is There A Plot in This Play?* Tuscaloosa: U of Alabama P, 1996.

Rorty, Richard. *Contingency, Irony, and Solidarity*. Cambridge: Cambridge UP, 1989.

Scheffler, Israel. *Science and Subjectivity*. Indianapolis: Bobbs, 1967.

Spigelman, Candace. "What Role Virtue?" *JAC* 21 (2001): 321–48.

Taylor, Charles. *Multiculturalism and "The Politics of Recognition": An Essay*. Ed. Amy Gutmann. Princeton: U of Princeton P, 1992.

White, James Boyd. *Heracles' Bow: Essays on the Rhetoric and Poetics of the Law*. Madison: U of Wisconsin P, 1985.

The Works of Stanley Fish

This bibliography comprises six sections: books, edited collections, book chapters, articles, reviews and commentary, and video and sound recordings. The entries in each section are arranged in reverse chronological order. Translations and interviews are not included. Parenthetical notes indicate when works later appeared in one of Fish's books; however, it is important to point out that frequently Fish substantially reworked and often renamed essays before including them in his books.

Books

How Milton Works. Cambridge: Harvard UP, 2001.

The Stanley Fish Reader. Ed. H. Aram Veeser. Malden, MA: Blackwell, 1999.

The Trouble with Principle. Cambridge: Harvard UP, 1999. (Reprinted in 2000 and 2001.)

Professional Correctness: Literary Studies and Political Change. Oxford: Clarendon, 1995. (Reprinted in 1999 by Harvard UP.)

There's No Such Thing as Free Speech, and It's a Good Thing, Too. New York: Oxford UP, 1994.

Doing What Comes Naturally: Change, Rhetoric, and the Practice of Theory in Literary and Legal Studies. Durham: Duke UP, 1989. (Reprinted in 1990 and 1999.)

Is There a Text in This Class? The Authority of Interpretive Communities. Cambridge: Harvard UP, 1980.

The Living Temple: George Herbert and Catechizing. Berkeley: U of California P, 1978.

Self-Consuming Artifacts: The Experience of Seventeenth-Century Literature. Berkeley: U of California P, 1972. (Reprinted in 1974 and 1994.)

Surprised by Sin: The Reader in Paradise Lost. New York: St. Martin's, 1967. (Reprinted in 1971 by U of California P and in 1997 and 1998 by Harvard UP.)

John Skelton's Poetry. New Haven: Yale UP, 1965. (Reprinted in 1976 by Archon Books.)

"The Poetry of Awareness: A Reassessment of John Skelton." Diss. Yale U, 1962.

Edited Collections

"A Renaissance Issue in Honor of Arnold Stein." Spec. Issue of *English Literary History* 49.2 (1982).

Seventeenth-Century Prose: Modern Essays in Criticism. New York: Oxford UP, 1971.

New Essays on Paradise Lost. Berkeley: U of California P, 1969.

Book Chapters

"Marvell and the Art of Disappearance." *Revenge of the Aesthetic: The Place of Literature in Theory Today.* Ed. Michael P. Clark. Berkeley: U of California P, 2000. 25–44.

"Professor Sokal's Bad Joke." *The Sokal Hoax: The Sham That Shook the Academy.* Ed. Editors of *Lingua Franca.* Lincoln: U of Nebraska P, 2000. 81–84.

"Masculine Persuasive Force: Donne and Verbal Power." *John Donne.* Ed. Andrew Mousley. New York: St. Martin's, 1999. 157–81.

"Interpreting the Variorum." *Contemporary Literary Criticism: Literary and Cultural Studies*. Ed. Robert Con Davis and Ronald Schleifer. New York: Longman, 1998. 182–96. (Chapter 6 of *Is There a Text in This Class?*)

"Rhetoric." *Rhetoric in an Antifoundational World: Language, Culture, and Pedagogy*. Ed. Michael Bernard-Donals and Richard R. Glejzer. New Haven: Yale UP, 1998. 33–64. (Chapter 20 of *Doing What Comes Naturally*.)

"Truth and Toilets: Pragmatism and the Practices of Life." *The Revival of Pragmatism: New Essays on Social Thought, Law, and Culture*. Ed. Morris Dickstein. Durham: Duke UP, 1998. 418–33. (Chapter 16 of *The Trouble With Principle*.)

"Consequences." *Twentieth-Century Literary Theory: A Reader*. Ed. K.M. Newton. New York: St. Martin's, 1997. 260–65. (Chapter 14 of *Doing What Comes Naturally*.)

"Interpreting the Variorum." *Twentieth-Century Literary Theory: A Reader*. Ed. K.M. Newton. New York: St. Martin's, 1997. 203–09. (Chapter 6 of *Is There a Text in This Class?*)

"Them We Burn: Violence and Conviction in the English Department." *English As a Discipline; or, Is There a Plot in This Play?* Ed. James C. Raymond. Tuscaloosa: U of Alabama P, 1996. 160–73.

"Working on the Chain Gang: Interpretation in Law and Literature." *Law and Literature: Text and Theory*. Ed. Lenora Ledwon. New York: Garland, 1996. 47–60. (Chapter 4 of *Doing What Comes Naturally*.)

"Things and Actions Indifferent: The Temptation of Plot in *Paradise Regained*." *Critical Essays on John Milton*. Ed. Christopher Kendrick. New York: G.K. Hall, 1995. 74–94.

"Is There a Text in This Class?" *Falling into Theory: Conflicting Views on Reading Literature*. Ed. David H. Richter and Gerald Graff. Boston: Bedford, 1994. 226–37. (Chapter 13 of *Is There a Text in This Class?*.)

"What Makes an Interpretation Acceptable?" *Contexts for Criticism*. Ed. Donald Keesey. Mountain View: Mayfield, 1994. 370–79. (Chapter 15 of *Is There a Text in This Class?*)

"The Common Touch, Or, One Size Fits All." *The Politics of Liberal Education*.

Ed. Darryl J. Gless and Barbara Hernstein Smith. Durham: Duke UP, 1992. 241–66. (Chapter 2 of *There's No Such Thing as Free Speech*.)

"Play of Surfaces: Theory and the Law." *Legal Hermeneutics: History, Theory, and Practice*. Ed. Gregory Leyh. Berkeley: U of California P, 1992. 297–316.

"There's No Such Thing as Free Speech and It's a Good Thing, Too." *Debating P.C.: The Controversy Over Political Correctness on College Campuses*. Ed. Paul Berman. New York: Laurel P, 1992. 231–45. (Chapter 8 of *There's No Such Thing As Free Speech*.)

"Almost Pragmatism: The Jurisprudence of Richard Posner, Richard Rorty, and Ronald Dworkin." *Pragmatism in Law and Society*. Ed. Michael Brint and William Weaver. Boulder: Westview, 1991. 47–81. (Chapter 13 of *There's No Such Thing as Free Speech*.)

"Biography and Intention." *Contesting the Subject: Essays in the Postmodern Theory and Practice of Biography and Biographical Criticism*. Ed. William H. Epstein. West Lafayette: Purdue UP, 1991. 9–16.

"The Law Wishes to Have a Formal Existence." *The Fate of Law*. Ed. Austin Sarat and Thomas R. Kearns. Ann Arbor: U of Michigan P, 1991. 159–208. (Chapter 11 of *There's No Such Thing As Free Speech*.)

"Masculine Persuasive Force: Donne and Verbal Power." *Soliciting Interpretation: Literary Theory and Seventeenth-Century English Poetry*. Ed. Elizabeth D. Harvey and Katharine Eisaman Maus. Chicago: U of Chicago P, 1990. 223–52.

"Wanting a Supplement: The Question of Interpretation in Milton's Early Prose." *Politics, Poetics, and Hermeneutics in Milton's Prose*. Ed. David Loewenstein and James Grantham Turner. Cambridge: Cambridge UP, 1990. 41–68. (Chapter 6 of *How Milton Works*.)

"Authors–Readers: Jonson's Community of the Same." *Representing the English Renaissance*. Ed. Stephen Greenblatt. Berkeley: U of California P, 1988. 231–64.

"Anti-Foundationalism, Theory Hope, and the Teaching of Composition." *The Current in Criticism: Essays on the Present and Future in Literary Theory*. Ed. Clayton Koelb and Virgil Lokke. West Lafayette: Purdue UP, 1987. 65–79. (Chapter 15 of *Doing What Comes Naturally*.)

"Driving From the Letter: Truth and Indeterminacy in Milton's 'Areopagitica.'" *Re-Membering Milton: Essays on the Texts and Traditions.* Ed. Mary Nyquist and Margaret W. Ferguson. New York: Methuen, 1987. 234–54. (Chapter 5 of *How Milton Works.*)

"Withholding the Missing Portion: Power, Meaning and Persuasion in Freud's The Wolf-Man." *The Linguistics of Writing: Arguments Between Language and Literature.* Ed. Nigel Fabb et al. New York: Methuen, 1987. 154–72. (Chapter 22 of *Doing What Comes Naturally.*)

"Transmuting the Lump: *Paradise Lost,* 1942–1982." *Literature and History: Theoretical Problems and Russian Case Studies.* Ed. Gary Saul Morson. Stanford: Stanford UP, 1986. 33–56. (Chapter 12 of *Doing What Comes Naturally.*)

"*Lycidas*: A Poem Finally Anonymous." *Milton's* Lycidas: *The Tradition and the Poem.* Ed. C.A. Patrides. Columbia: U of Missouri P, 1983. 319–40. (Chapter 7 of *How Milton Works.*)

"How To Recognize a Poem When You See One." *American Criticism in the Poststructuralist Age.* Ed. Ira Konigsberg. Ann Arbor: U of Michigan P, 1981. 102–15. (Chapter 14 of *Is There a Text in This Class?*)

"Persuasion vs. Demonstration, or How Can You Tell the Name of the Game if the Game Is Always Changing?" *What Is Criticism.* Ed. Paul Hernadi. Bloomington: Indiana UP, 1981. 30–37. (Chapter 16 of *Is There a Text in This Class?*)

"Problem Solving in *Comus.*" *Illustrious Evidence: Approaches to English Literature of the Early Seventeenth Century.* Ed. Earl Miner. Berkeley: U of California P, 1975. 115–31. (Chapter 3 of *How Milton Works.*)

"Catechizing the Reader: Herbert's Socratean Rhetoric." *The Rhetoric of Renaissance Poetry from Wyatt to Milton.* Ed. Thomas O. Sloan and Raymond B. Waddington. Berkeley: U of California P, 1974. 174–88.

"What Is Stylistics and Why Are They Saying Such Terrible Things About It?" *Approaches to Poetics: Selected Papers from the English Institute.* Ed. Seymour Chatman. New York: Columbia UP, 1973. 109–52. (Chapter 2 of *Is There a Text in This Class?*)

"The Harassed Reader in *Paradise Lost.*" *Milton:* Paradise Lost, *A Casebook.* Ed. A.E. Dyson, Julian Lovelock. London: Macmillan, 1973. 152–78.

"Sequence and Meaning in Seventeenth-Century Narrative." *To Tell a Story: Narrative Theory and Practice*. Ed. Earl Miner and Robert M. Adams. Los Angeles: Wm. Andrews Clark Memorial Lib., 1973. 59–76. (Papers read at a Clark Library Seminar, February 4, 1972.)

"Georgics of the Mind: Bacon's Philosophy and the Experience of His Essays." *English Literature and British Philosophy: A Collection of Essays*. Ed. S.P. Rosenbaum. Chicago: U of Chicago P, 1971. 15–39.

"Inaction and Silence: The Reader in *Paradise Regained*." *Calm of Mind: Tercentenary Essays on* Paradise Regained *and* Samson Agonistes *in Honor of John S. Diekhoff*. Ed. Joseph A. Wittreich, Jr. et al. Cleveland: P of Case Western Reserve U, 1971. 25–47. (Chapter 10 of *How Milton Works*.)

"Reasons That Imply Themselves: Imagery, Argument, and the Reader in Milton's *Reason of Church Government*." *Seventeenth-Century Imagery: Essays on Uses of Figurative Language from Donne to Farquhar*. Ed. Earl Miner. Berkeley: U of California P, 1971. 83–102.

"Discovery as Form in *Paradise Lost*." *New Essays on* Paradise Lost. Ed. Thomas Kranidas. Berkeley: U of California P, 1969. 1–14.

Articles

"Condemnation without Absolutes; Postmodernism and the Reality of Terrorism." *New York Times* 15 Oct. 2001: A19.

"Holocaust Denial and Academic Freedom." *Valparaiso University Law Review* 35.3 (2001): 499–524.

"Pith and Pea-filled Bladders." *Chicago Tribune* 22 July 2001, sec. 2:1+.

"To Thine Own Faculty Be Truthful." *Chronicle of Higher Education*. 19 Oct. 2001, sec. 2: B13–14.

"The Invisible Professor." *Across the Board* 38.3 (2001): 13.

"Fisheye: A Sneaky Kind of Censorship." *Across the Board* 37.8 (2000): 10.

"Nice Work If You Can Get Them to Do It." *ADE Bulletin* 126 (2000): 15–17.

"The Nifty Nine Arguments Against Affirmative Action in Higher Education." Journal of Blacks in Higher Education 27 (2000): 79–81.

"Reverse Racism, or How The Pot Got to Call The Kettle Black." *New Crisis* 107 (2000): 14–21. (Chapter 4 of *There's No Such Thing as Free Speech*.)

"Theory Minimalism." *San Diego Law Review* 37 (2000): 761–76.

"The High-Minded Fight Over Florida." *New York Times* 15 Nov. 2000, late ed.: A29.

"Running Away from a Daunting Television Legacy." *New York Times* 22 Oct. 2000, late ed.: AR27.

"Academic Freedom: When Sauce for the Goose Isn't Sauce for the Gander." *Chronicle of Higher Education* 26 Nov. 1999: B4–6. (Chapter 2 of *The Trouble With Principle*.)

"Interpretation Is Not a Theoretical Issue." *Yale Journal of Law and the Humanities* 11 (1999): 507–14.

"Just Published: Minutiae Without Meaning." *New York Times* 7 Sept. 1999: A19+.

"A Reply to J. Judd Owen." *American Political Science Review* 93 (1999): 925–30.

"Boutique Multiculturalism, or Why Liberals are Incapable of Thinking About Hate Speech." *Critical Inquiry* 23 (1997): 378–96. (Chapter 4 of *The Trouble With Principle*.)

"Mission Impossible: Settling the Just Bounds Between Church and State." *Columbia Law Review* 97 (1997): 2255–333. (Chapters 9, 10, and 11 of *The Trouble With Principle*.)

"School for the Scandalous." *New York Times* 21 Nov. 1997: A27+.

"Children and the First Amendment." *Connecticut Law Review* 29 (1997): 883–92. (Chapter 8 of *The Trouble With Principle*.)

"At the Federalist Society." *Howard Law Journal* 39 (1996): 719–35. (Chapter 1 of *The Trouble With Principle*.)

"Professor Sokal's Bad Joke." *New York Times* 21 May 1996: A23+.

"A Reply to Richard John Neuhaus." *First Things: A Monthly Journal of Religion and Public Life* 60 (1996): 35–40. (Chapter 13 of *The Trouble With Principle*.)

"When Principles Get in the Way." *New York Times* 26 Dec. 1996: A27+.

"Why We Can't All Just Get Along." *First Things: A Monthly Journal of Religion and Public Life* 60 (1996): 18–26. (Chapter 12 of *The Trouble With Principle.*)

"How the Right Hijacked the Magic Words." *New York Times* 13 Aug. 1995, sec. 4: Op-Ed. ("Epilogue" of *The Trouble With Principle.*)

"With Mortal Voice: Milton Defends Against the Muse." *English Literary History* 62 (1995): 509–27. (Chapter 8 of *How Milton Works.*)

"Spin Lawyers: Arguments in Current Cases are an Exercise in Doublespeak." *Los Angeles Daily Journal* 18 Aug. 1995: 6 col 3.

"What It Means to Do a Job of Work." *English Literary Renaissance* 25 (1995): 354–71.

"Affirmative Action and the SAT." *Journal of Blacks in Higher Education* 2 (1993–94): 83.

Fish, Stanley E., et al. "Is Diversity Training Worth Maintaining?" *Business and Society Review* 89 (1994): 47–49.

"Fraught With Death: Skepticism, Progressivism, and the First Amendment." *University of Colorado Law Review* 64 (1993): 1061–086. (Chapter 6 of *The Trouble With Principle.*)

"How Come You Do Me Like You Do? A Response to Dennis Patterson." *Texas Law Review* 72 (1993): 57–77.

"Ivory-Tower Masochists." *Harper's Magazine* Sept. 1993: 20–21.

"Martyrs to a Higher Cause." *Times Higher Education Supplement* 16 Apr. 1993: 17.

"Not of an Age, But for All Time: Canons and Postmodernism." *Journal of Legal Education* 43.1 (1993): 11–21. (Chapter 3 of *The Trouble With Principle.*)

"On Legal Autonomy." *Mercer Law Review* 44 (1993): 737–41.

"Reverse Racism, or, How the Pot Got to Call the Kettle Black." *Atlantic Monthly* Nov. 1993: 128–33. (Chapter 4 of *There's No Such Thing as Free Speech.*)

"Bad Company." *Transition* 56 (1992): 60–67. (Chapter 6 of *There's No Such Thing as Free Speech*.)

"Being Interdisciplinary Is So Very Hard to Do." *Profession 89* (1989): 15–22. (Chapter 14 of *There's No Such Thing As Free Speech*.)

Leak, Gary K., and Stanley E. Fish. "Religious Orientation, Impression Management, and Self-Deception: Toward a Clarification of the Link between Religiosity and Social Desirability." *Journal for the Scientific Study of Religion* 28 (1989): 355–59.

"Spectacle and Evidence in Samson Agonistes." *Critical Inquiry* 15 (1989): 556–86. (Chapter 13 of *How Milton Works*.)

"Critical Legal Studies (II): Roberto Unger's Transformative Politics." *Raritan* 7.3 (1988): 1–24. (Chapter 18 of *Doing What Comes Naturally*.)

"Don't Know Much About the Middle Ages: Posner on Law and Literature." *Yale Law Journal* 97 (1988): 777–93. (Chapter 13 of *Doing What Comes Naturally*.)

"Force." *Washington and Lee Law Review* 45 (1988): 883-902. (Chapter 21 of *Doing What Comes Naturally*.)

"No Bias, No Merit: The Case Against Blind Submission." *PMLA* 103 (1988): 739–48. (Chapter 8 of *Doing What Comes Naturally*.)

"Unger and Milton." *Duke Law Journal* 5 (1988): 975–1012. (Chapter 18 of *Doing What Comes Naturally*.)

"Change." *South Atlantic Quarterly* 86 (1987): 423–44. (Chapter 7 of *Doing What Comes Naturally*.)

"Critical Legal Studies: Unger and Milton." *Raritan* 7.2 (1987): 1–20. (Chapter 18 of *Doing What Comes Naturally*.)

"Dennis Martinez and the Uses of Theory." *Yale Law Journal* 96 (1987): 1773–800. (Chapter 17 of *Doing What Comes Naturally*.)

"Liberalism Doesn't Exist." *Duke Law Journal* 5 (1987): 997–1001.

"Still Wrong After All These Years." *Law and Philosophy* 6 (1987): 401–18. (Chapter 16 of *Doing What Comes Naturally*.)

Anti-Professionalism. *Cardozo Law Review* 7 (1986): 645–77. (Chapter 11 of *Doing What Comes Naturally*.)

"Withholding the Missing Portion: Power, Meaning and Persuasion." *Times Literary Supplement* (1986): 935–38. (Chapter 22 of *Doing What Comes Naturally*.)

"Anti-Professionalism." *New Literary History* 17 (1985): 89–127. (Chapter 11 of *Doing What Comes Naturally*.)

"Consequences." *Critical Inquiry* 11 (1985): 433–58. (Chapter 14 of *Doing What Comes Naturally*.)

"Resistance and Independence: A Reply to Gerald Graff." *New Literary History* 17 (1985): 119–27.

"Theory Is Without Consequence." *Critique* 41 (1985): 445–69.

"Author–Readers: Jonson's Community of the Same." *Representations* 7 (1984): 26–58.

"Fear of Fish: A Reply to Walter Davis." *Critical Inquiry* 10 (1984): 695–705.

"Fish v. Fiss." *Sanford Law Review* 36 (1984): 1325–347. (Chapter 6 of *Doing What Comes Naturally*.)

"Fish v. Fiss." *Mississippi College Law Review* 5 (1984): 1–23. (Chapter 6 of *Doing What Comes Naturally*.)

"Profession Despise Thyself: Fear and Self-Loathing in Literary Studies." *Critical Inquiry* 10 (1983): 349–73. (Chapter 10 of *Doing What Comes Naturally*.)

"A Reply to Eugene Goodheart." *Daedalus* 112.1 (1983): 233–37.

"Short People Got No Reason to Live: Reading Irony." *Daedalus* 112 (1983): 175–91. (Chapter 9 of *Doing What Comes Naturally*.)

"Things and Actions Indifferent: The Temptation of Plot in *Paradise Regained*." *Milton Studies* 17 (1983): 163–85. (Chapter 11 of *How Milton Works*.)

"Wrong Again." *Texas Law Review* 62 (1983): 299–316. (Chapter 5 of *Doing What Comes Naturally*.)

"With the Compliments of the Author: Reflections on Austin and Derrida." *Critical Inquiry* 8 (1982): 693–791. (Chapter 2 of *Doing What Comes Naturally*.)

"Interpretation and the Pluralist Vision." *Texas Law Review* 60 (1982): 495–505.

"Working on the Chain Gang: Interpretation in Law and Literature." *Texas Law Review* 60 (1982): 551–67. (Chapter 4 of *Doing What Comes Naturally*.)

"Working on the Chain Gang: Interpretation in the Law and in Literary Criticism." *Critical Inquiry* 9 (1982): 201–16. (Chapter 4 of *Doing What Comes Naturally*.)

Fish, Stanley E., et al. "Professing Literature: A Symposium on the Study of English." *Times Literary Supplement* 10 Dec. 1982: 1355–363.

"*Lycidas*: A Poem Finally Anonymous." *Glyph* 8 (1981): 1–18. (Chapter 7 of *How Milton Works*.)

"The Temptation to Action in Milton's Poetry." *English Literary History* 48 (1981): 516–31. (Chapter 9 of *How Milton Works*.)

"Why No One's Afraid of Wolfgang Iser." *Diacritics* 11 (1981): 2–13. (Chapter 3 of *Doing What Comes Naturally*.)

"Reply to John Reichert's 'Making Sense of Interpretation.'" *Critical Inquiry* 6 (1980): 749–51.

"A Reply to John Reichert; or, How to Stop Worrying and Learn to Love Interpretation." *Critical Inquiry* 6 (1979): 173–78. (Chapter 12 of *Is There a Text in This Class?*)

"What Is Stylistics and Why Are They Saying Such Terrible Things About It? Part II." *Boundary 2* 8 (1979): 129–45. (Chapter 10 of *Is There a Text in This Class?*)

"Normal Circumstances, Literal Language, Direct Speech Acts, the Ordinary, the Everyday, the Obvious, What Goes Without Saying, and Other Special Cases." *Critical Inquiry* 4 (1978): 625–44. (Chapter 11 of *Is There a Text in This Class?*)

"Doing Scholarship: The Mystery of *The Temple* Finally Explained." *George Herbert Journal* 1 (1977): 1–9.

"How to Do Things with Austin and Searle: Speech-Act Theory and Literary Criticism."*Modern Language Notes* 91 (1976): 983–1025. (Chapter 9 of *Is There a Text in This Class?*)

"Interpreting the Variorum." *Critical Inquiry* 2 (1976): 465–85. (Chapter 6 of *Is There a Text in This Class?*)

"Interpreting 'Interpreting the Variorum.'" *Critical Inquiry* 3 (1976): 191–96. (Chapter 6 of *Is There a Text in This Class?*)

"Structuralist Homiletics." *Modern Language Notes* 91 (1976): 1208–221. (Chapter 8 of *Is There a Text in This Class?*)

"Facts and Fictions: A Reply to Ralph Rader." *Critical Inquiry* 1 (1975): 883–91. (Chapter 5 of *Is There a Text in This Class?*)

"Speech-Act Theory, Literary Criticism, and *Coriolanus*." *Centrum: Working Papers of the Minnesota Center for Advanced Studies in Language, Style, and Literary Theory* 3 (1975): 107–11.

"What It's Like to Read *L'Allegro* and *Il Penseroso*." *Milton Studies* 7 (1975): 77–99. (Chapter 4 of *Is There a Text in This Class?*)

"How Ordinary Is Ordinary Language?" *New Literary History* 5 (1973): 41–54. (Chapter 3 of *Is There a Text in This Class?*)

"Recent Studies in the English Renaissance." *SEL: Studies in English Literature, 1500–1900* 12 (1972): 183–222.

"Georgics of the Mind: The Experience of Bacon's Essays." *Critical Quarterly* 13 (1971): 45–68.

"Progress in *The Pilgrim's Progress*." *English Literary Renaissance* 1 (1971): 261–93.

"Things and Actions Indifferent: The Temptation of Plot in *Paradise Regained*." *Milton Studies* 17 (1971): 163–85. (Chapter 11 of *How Milton Works*.)

"Letting Go: The Reader in Herbert's Poetry." *English Literary History* 37 (1970): 475–94.

"Literature in the Reader: Affective Stylistics." *New Literary History* 2 (1970): 123–62. (Chapter 1 of *Is There a Text in This Class?*)

"Question and Answer in *Samson Agonistes*." *Critical Quarterly* 11 (1969): 237–64. (Chapter 12 of *How Milton Works*.)

"Standing Only: Christian Heroism in *Paradise Lost*." *Critical Quarterly* 9 (1967): 162–78.

"Milton's God: Two Defences and a Qualification." *Southern Review* (1966–67): 116–36.

"Further Thoughts on Milton's Christian Reader." *Critical Quarterly* 7 (1965): 279–84.

"The Harassed Reader in *Paradise Lost*." *Critical Quarterly* 7 (1965): 162–82.

"Nature as Concept and Character in the 'Mutabilitie Cantos.'" *College Language Association Journal* 6 (1963): 210–15.

"Aspects of Rhetorical Analysis: Skelton's 'Philip Sparrow.'" *Studia Neophilologica* 34 (1962): 216–38.

"*The Nun's Priest's Tale* and Its Analogues." *College Language Association Journal* 5 (1962): 223–28.

Reviews and Commentary

Rev. of *Impartiality in Context: Grounding Justice in a Pluralist World* by Shane O'Neill. *Jurist: The Legal Education Network*. Oct. 1998. http://www.jurist.law.pitt.edu/lawbooks/revoct98.htm.

Rev. of *Before the Shooting Begins* by James Davison Hunger. *Washington Times* 10 Apr. 1994: B8+.

Rev. of *Imposters in the Temple* by Martin Anderson. *Washington Monthly* Sept. 1992: 53–55.

Rev. of *The Problems of Jurisprudence* by Richard A. Posner. *University of Chicago Law Review* 57 (1990): 1447–475.

"The Young and the Restless." *The New Historicism*. Ed. H. Aram Veeser. New York: Routledge, 1989. 303–16.

Commentary on "Literary Theory in the University: A Survey." *New Literary History* 14 (1983): 418.

Rev. of *The Christian Poet in* Paradise Lost by William G. Riggs. *Modern Philology* 72 (1974): 194–97.

Rev. of *The Languages of Literature: Some Linguistic Contributions to Criticism* by Roger Fowler. *Linguistics* 141 (1974): 79–83.

Rev. of *The Prison House of Language: A Critical Account of Structuralism and Russian Formalism* by Frederic Jameson *Novel* 6 (1973): 283–87.

Rev. of *Spenser and Literary Pictorialism* by John B. Bender. *Medievalia et Humanistica* 4 (1973): 239–41.

Video and Sound Recordings

Fish, Stanley E., et al. *Legal Scholarship in the Humanities: The View from inside the Triangle.* Audiocassette. Recorded Resources Corp., 1999.

The Trouble with Principle; Hate Speech and Liberal Proceduralism. Tenth Belle R. and Joseph H. Braun Memorial Distinguished Lecture. Videocassette. 1999.

Fish, Stanley E., et al. *Yahoo!* Soundings Series. CD. Natl. Humanities Center, 1997.

Fish, Stanley E., et al. *Affirmative Action: The History of an Idea.* Democracy Project Series. Videocassette. Films for the Humanities, 1996.

Fish, Stanley E., et al. *Pornography.* "Linda Belans Show." Audiocassette. WUNC Radio, 1996.

Fish, Stanley E., et al. *Teachers In Cyberspace.* CD. Natl. Humanities Center, 1996.

Living With The Fall: Milton's Paradise Lost. Duke Great Teachers Series. Videocassette. Public Media Education, 1994.

Fish, Stanley E., et al. *Stanley Steamers.* CD. Natl. Humanities Center, 1993.

Fish, Stanley E., et al. *Famine, Farming, and Flowers* and *There's No Such Thing As Free Speech.* LP. Natl. Humanities Center, 1992.

Fish, Stanley E., et al. *Leading Communists.* LP. Natl. Humanities Center, 1992.

Fish, Stanley E., et al. *Political Correctness, Multi-Culturalism, and Hate Speech on Campus.* Videocassette. Duke U, 1991.

Fish, Stanley E., et al. *British Imperialism and Native Cultures.* LP. Natl. Humanities Center, 1990.

Fish, Stanley E., et al. *The Imperial Presence;* and *Doing What Comes Naturally.* LP. Natl. Humanities Center, 1990.

Force. The John Randolph Tucker Lecture. Videocassette. Washington and Lee U, 1988. (Chapter 21 of *Doing What Comes Naturally.*)

Fish, Stanley E., et al. *Convergence in Crisis: Narratives of the History of Theory.* Audiocassette. Duke U, 1988.

Fish, Stanley E., et al. *Earth and Other Ethics.* LP. Natl. Humanities Center, 1988.

Change. Patten Foundation Lectures. Audiocassette. Indiana U, 1987.

Critical Self-Consciousness, or, Can We Know What We're Doing. Patten Foundation Lectures. Audiocassette. Indiana U, 1987.

Fish, Stanley E., et al. *Literary Criticism 1984: Interpretation, the Critical Difference.* Audiocassette. Georgetown U, 1984.

Fish, Stanley E., et al. *Symposium on Literary Criticism.* Audiotape. U of Tennessee, 1978.

How to Stop Worrying by Stopping Reading. Fourth Diacritics Colloquium. Audiocassette. Cornell U, 1976.

Index